MISSING FROM POND VIEW

I0102102

Readers are encouraged to go to www.MissionPointPress.com to contact the author or to find information on how to buy this book in bulk at a discounted rate.

Published by Mission Point Press
2554 Chandler Lake Rd.
Traverse City, MI 49686
(231) 421-9513
www.MissionPointPress.com

ISBN: 978-1-950659-22-7
Library of Congress Control Number: 2019913984
Printed in the United States of America.

MISSING FROM POND VIEW

A MYSTERY BY
STUART SAFFT

MISSION POINT PRESS

Author's Note

My special thanks go to Joey Tucker for his time and patience in helping me understand the inner workings of drug task forces. Joey retired from the South Carolina Highway Patrol after twenty-five years of service. As First Sergeant, he had day-to-day responsibility for Patrol operations in one of the state's largest counties and also served as Assistant Troop Commander for Troop Three and as a sergeant. While a Trooper, Joey was a member of the Highway Patrol SWAT Team and served on the DEA drug task force in South Carolina. Joey, many thanks — I hope I didn't mess things up too badly.

Chapter 1

"**M**ondays are killers," said Joe McFarland to Ginny Harris, his professional and personal partner, sitting opposite him at her desk at the Jasper Creek Police Department.

"Tell me about it. We did nothing all weekend, and I'm exhausted."

"I'm glad there's not much going on. It's not often I'm happy to be chained to my desk all day, catching up on paperwork. Beside it being Monday, it's cold as hell out there."

"Joe, it's not cold as hell — it's cold as you'd expect early March in Ohio to be. But, if you're asking if I'm ready for spring, my answer is a big, fat yes."

"Hey, Joe. Ginny. You guys got a minute?" bellowed the chief all the way from his office doorway at the far end of the room.

"Uh-oh," said Joe. "I knew it was too good to last."

As Joe and Ginny got up from their desks and walked to the chief's office, several detectives in the room smiled and a few whispered teasing comments to Joe and Ginny. "Bad, bad, bad." "Called to the principal's office again." "Joe, how'd you screw up this time?" "You shoulda known you couldn't get away with it."

"Yeah, yeah," mumbled Joe as he and Ginny made their way across the room.

"What's up, Chief?" asked Ginny as they reached the chief's office.

"Got a case for you. Come on in."

Joe and Ginny walked into the office and sat down on the two small chairs in front of the chief's desk.

"Pond View," said the chief as he settled into his chair behind the desk.

"Same to you," responded Joe with a smile. "Like to tell us a little more?"

"Pond View Girls Academy. The fancy, and expensive, girls boarding school out on Martin Avenue, up in the northwest corner."

"I'm aware of the school, Chief," said Ginny. "I did grow up here, you know."

"Well, one of their students has gone missing. Need you guys to head out there and start digging. Hopefully, it's nothing and she just ran off for a short burst of freedom. But you never know."

"OK," said Joe. "Who called it in? How long ago?"

"A Ms. Franley. She's head of the school. 9-1-1 got the call about 30 minutes ago."

"Got it," said Ginny. "Give us five minutes to straighten out the piles on our desks, and we're on our way."

"I'm guessing this'll be a wild goose chase, but I know — we have to check it out. We'll probably stop for lunch on the way back, and then we'll fill you in."

"OK. Thanks," said the chief as he picked up a pen and focused his attention on the stack of papers on his desk, acting as if Joe and Ginny were no longer there.

Joe and Ginny got the hint, left the chief's office and headed back to their desks.

Ten minutes later they were in Joe's car, pulling out of the PD parking lot.

"Ginny, how come you didn't go to this school?"

"It cost a bloody fortune. My parents couldn't come close to being able to pay for it. Don't know exactly what it cost back then, but it's about sixty grand a year now. And now they have a lot of scholarships and loans that didn't exist back in the day."

"Sixty thou. Wow! That's more than most colleges."

"Yeah. But it's a top junior high and high school for girls. Virtually all the students get into college, many of them into the best ones. So it's probably a good investment, but if you can't afford it, you can't afford it."

"Gotcha."

Twenty minutes later, Joe pulled into one of the visitors' parking spaces directly in front of the administration building. Joe was surprised by the campus. He had driven past the school several times, but never actually driven into the campus. It looked like a small New England town. A few larger buildings housed the administration, classrooms and laboratories, library, dining room and physical education facilities. About a dozen smaller buildings, mostly three-story houses, served as the dormitories. In front of two of the largest buildings was a large open area, with several students walking between buildings. The grassy areas remained snow-covered, but the walkways had been plowed and shoveled clean.

Joe and Ginny entered the building marked Administration, identified themselves to the receptionist and asked to see Franley. The receptionist immediately led them down the hall and into Franley's office.

"Good morning, Detectives. Thank you for coming so promptly. Please sit down. May I offer you some coffee or tea?"

Joe thought how Franley looked exactly as he expected. *Probably in her mid-50s. Tall, thin and severe looking, with her hair pinned in some type of bun at the back of her head. Her white blouse and dark gray skirt fit perfectly with her makeup-free face. Clearly a principal or librarian type.*

Joe and Ginny both went for black coffee. Coffees in hand, they sat on a plush couch in one corner of Franley's large office, with Franley sitting on an identical couch on the opposite side of the coffee table.

"Ms. Franley, please fill us in. We understand one of your students is missing."

"Yes, yes, that's true. I can't believe it."

"Please walk us through the details. How and when you first learned she was missing? What you did? Where you've already checked? Who else you got involved in looking for her? Anything we should know about her? And so on," said Ginny.

"I got a call about eight-thirty this morning from Mrs. Porter. She's our dean of students. Seems that Amy Richardson hasn't been seen for two days. Since Saturday morning. Mrs. Porter had called her parents, but they hadn't seen or heard from her in a week. That's when I called 9-1-1."

"Does Amy have a roommate? Any close friends here? We'd like to speak with them. Also, with whoever saw her last. Plus Mrs. Porter, as well as your head of security. Then Amy's parents, of course," said Ginny.

"No problem. I'll have my assistant take you to Mrs. Porter's office. While you're there, I'll arrange for Miss Kendall to meet with you. She's the house director of Hurst Hall. That's where Amy's room is. Then you should come back here. I'll alert Victor Denton that you'll want to talk with him. He's our facilities manager and also looks after security." She wrote on a piece of paper and handed it to Ginny. "Here's Amy's parents' address and phone number. They live nearby in Avon."

After an awkward moment of silence, Franley said, "Uh, there's one other thing."

"Yes?" said Joe.

"Until we're sure exactly what's going on and what, if anything, happened to Amy, we'd like to keep this quiet. We don't want to upset our other students or any of the other parents unnecessarily."

"We understand," said Joe. "We'll do what we can. But we can't promise anything. Our first priority is Amy, and we'll do whatever we feel is necessary. Not upsetting the other students or parents, or not tarnishing the school's reputation and image, can't be our first priority."

"Yes, yes, of course. I understand. But whatever you can do would be most appreciated by me and our board of trustees."

Ginny and Joe gave Franley their business cards and followed her to her assistant, Nancy Jenkins. After introductions, Jenkins led Joe and Ginny to Porter's office.

From an appearance standpoint, Porter was almost the complete opposite of Franley: about 20 years younger, bleached blonde hair, bright lipstick complementing her brightly colored blouse and slacks.

Joe and Ginny sat in two of the chairs in front of Porter's desk.

Ginny started right in. "Mrs. Porter, can you tell us how you found out that Amy Richardson was missing?"

"Yes, sure. Barbara Kendall, she's the house director of Amy's dorm, called me at home this morning. About 7:45. She realized she hadn't seen Amy since Saturday morning. She checked with Amy's roommate, who said that Amy hadn't slept in her room Saturday or Sunday night. The roommate said Amy hadn't mentioned anything, but she assumed that Amy had gone home for the weekend. I then called Amy's parents and learned that wasn't the case. Needless to say, her parents weren't happy."

"Then what did you do?" ask Ginny.

"I immediately called Ms. Franley. She doesn't like to be caught off guard when anything unusual happens."

"Mrs. Porter, do you have any idea where Amy might have gone or what might have happened to her?" asked Joe.

"Happened to her? Do you think something bad happened?"

"We have no idea," said Joe. "At this point, we have to be open to any and all possibilities."

"Yes, I can understand that. But I'd be surprised if it wasn't like the other times."

"The other times?" asked Ginny.

"Please, don't get me wrong. Amy's a very sweet girl. And very intelligent. But she has a spoiled, or perhaps rebellious, streak in her. Amy's a junior this year. This is her third year with us and she's been living in my dorm all three years. She's taken off for a day or two without permission before. Probably two or three times a year."

"Oh. This is the first we've heard about that," said Ginny. "Any idea where she went the other times?"

"No. She'd never tell us. Or her parents. She's been on probation a couple of times for these absences, but she's smart enough to wait until her probation ends before running off again."

"Any reason to think it's anything different this time?" asked Joe.

"Not really. Except…"

"Yes? Except what?" prompted Joe.

"Best I can remember, this is the first time she wasn't back in time for her first Monday morning class. Maybe she just overslept someplace, or somehow got delayed returning."

"How'd she normally travel when she left in the past?"

"No idea. Our students aren't allowed cars here. Maybe she stayed real local. Or someone picked her up. Or maybe she took a bus or taxi."

Joe and Ginny thanked Porter and gave her their cards, after which the receptionist, after bundling herself in coat, scarf, hat and gloves, escorted them a few buildings over to Hurst Hall, where they met first with Barbara Kendall, house director of Amy's dorm, and then with Carol Davis, Amy's roommate. Neither shed any additional light on the situation. Davis stated that she and Amy were quite close, having roomed together all three years. Davis did confirm, however, that she never had any advance knowledge of Amy's disappearances, nor did Amy ever explain after the fact where she had gone or why.

Joe and Ginny returned to the administration building and found their way to Victor Denton's office. Their short discussion provided nothing useful.

"My real job is taking care of all the facilities here — buildings, equipment, vehicles, roads and so on. They added security to my load a few years ago."

"Can you describe the security organization for us?" asked Ginny.

"'Organization' is too big a word for what we do. Have a few part-time guards reporting to me, usually one during the day and two at night. But they're nothing like a campus police force — we're too small for that. Their uniformed presence probably keeps some troublemakers away. Any crime-like things we call you guys. These folks are first responders for accidents, injuries or, God forbid, fires. They handle parking issues and any minor squabbles among the students. But that's about it."

"Did you or they see anything the day Amy Richardson went missing."

"Nope. I wasn't here that day, and I already asked the guard who was on duty. Nothing."

"How about surveillance videos?"

"Sorry. We don't have any. We've talked about them, but budgets keep getting in the way."

Joe and Ginny thanked Denton and walked back to Franley's office to close the loop with her. They expressed their displeasure at not having been told of Amy's history of running away. Ginny asked Franley for the dates of

Amy's prior disappearances. Franley said that she would check their records and get the dates to Ginny before the end of the day. Joe said they were going to visit Amy's parents next. He indicated that, although they would continue to treat this as a missing persons case, they were tentatively viewing it as another runaway episode from which Amy would shortly return.

On the way to Avon to speak with Amy's parents, Ginny called the desk sergeant and arranged for a few uniformed officers to canvas the school grounds and surrounding neighborhood and to check for surveillance cameras within a five-block radius of the school. Hopefully, someone saw how Amy left — or was taken away. Or even better, her departure was captured on a surveillance camera. She also arranged for a few officers to search the nearby pond for which the school was named and the small wooded area surrounding it.

Joe swerved into an IHOP restaurant they were about to pass. "OK, Ginny. A special treat for lunch today. All kinds of pancakes and choices of syrup. About as close to heaven as you can get around here."

"Joe, with all the calories we're about to gobble up we'll never be able to even lift off the ground, much less get all the way up to heaven."

"Well I, for one, am willing to risk it."

"Why aren't I the least bit surprised?" asked Ginny with a smile.

Despite it being lunchtime, Joe went with two eggs, bacon and a side of pancakes. Ginny selected a small stack of buckwheat pancakes, and both had black coffee.

Feeling stuffed, they were soon again on their way to Amy's parents.

Joe pulled into the circular driveway in front of Amy's house. 'Mansion' might be a better term than house. A large, white, two-story building with a series of columns along the porch which ran the entire length of the house. The property was large, probably close to two acres. Although a blanket of snow covered the lawn, it was clear that the bushes and trees were immaculately trimmed. Joe and Ginny walked up to the bright blue front door and rang the bell. Almost immediately, a housemaid, in black uniform with a short white apron, opened the door. Joe and Ginny were soon sitting with Amy's parents in the sunroom at the rear of the house.

Joe and Ginny spent about twenty minutes with Mr. and Mrs. Richardson. Having learned of Amy's history of running away, Joe and Ginny weren't surprised that Amy's parents were more upset with her than worried about her. They fully expected her to show up back at school at any moment. Although readily admitting that Amy was at fault for running off, Mr. Richardson also was highly critical of the school. "Heck, they know she's run off several times. You'd think they'd care enough to pay a bit more attention to her comings and goings. You don't have to be a rocket scientist to expect she might try to run off again."

Other than that, Amy's parents had little to offer regarding where Amy might have gone and, if not alone, with whom. They reiterated their belief that Amy would soon return, but nonetheless thanked Ginny and Joe for their efforts in trying to find her.

Joe and Ginny requested and received a detailed description of Amy. They gave the parents their business cards and said their good-byes, after which they drove back to Jasper Creek and parked in the lot behind the department. They went right to the chief's office, summarized their interviews and expressed their opinion that this was most likely nothing more than the latest of Amy's runaways.

"And that's it, Chief," Ginny said. "She'll probably show up back at school in a day or two."

"Good work," said the chief. "I know I don't have to remind you that, despite your tentative conclusions and expectations — which, by the way, are most likely correct, you need to be sure not to write up your notes that way. Just in case this turns out to be something more serious, we don't need the negative publicity of having written this off as a spoiled rich kid's rebellion."

"No need to tell us, Chief. We know the drill," said Joe.

"OK. Thanks. Joe, I'd like to talk with you for a minute," said the chief as he looked at Joe and then glanced at Ginny, obviously awaiting her departure.

"Uh, yeah, sure. I'll head back. I want to check with the taxi companies to see if one of them might have picked Amy up from school. Then I'll start writing our report. See you in a few, Joe." Ginny was clearly taken aback by being so abruptly asked to leave. Up until this incident, the chief had always pretty much treated Joe and her as equal members of a team, dealing with them together. But she hid her surprise well, got up, left the office and closed the door behind her.

Chapter 2

"**W**hat's up, Chief?"

"Joe, what I'm going to tell you is very confidential. You can't share it with anyone. And I mean anyone. Except, of course, Ginny."

"OK. Let's have it. What's this top secret?"

"Joe, we want to assign you to a drug enforcement task force."

"Chief! Jeez! You know how I hate task forces. I served on enough of them when I was with Chicago PD to last me a couple of lifetimes — armed robbery, violent gang, human trafficking. Not drug task forces, but they're all the same."

"Joe, this one is very important. And your assignment on this drug task force will be different than those you've had in the past."

"Come on, Chief. Gimme a break. I know the arguments all too well. Drug addiction kills way more people than guns and knives. Profits from the drug trade finance all kinds of other criminal enterprises. The drug traffickers are so widespread and sophisticated that only a high-level, multi-agency task force has any chance to win the battle. How am I doing so far?"

"You have all the right arguments for these task forces, but you —"

"Now let me tell you how these task forces really work.

The member agencies are more focused on winning points and getting credit than they are on beating the bad guys. And the individuals they assign to the task forces, more often than not, are those they don't have a place for in their own organization, but aren't quite incompetent enough to be fired. Everybody on the task force wants to be a leader and no one wants to do any of the heavy lifting."

"OK, Joe. Feeling better after having spewed all that out? Now how about just listening for a couple of minutes… think that's possible?"

"Uh, yeah, sure. I'm all ears."

"This is part of the DEA's State and Local Task Force Program. Specifically, it's the High Intensity Drug Trafficking Area task force covering the counties around Cleveland. That's from Lake Erie south to Medina County, Akron and Youngstown. Then it runs north along the Pennsylvania border back up to the lake."

"I get it. Like the northeast corner of the state."

"Very good with the geography exam, Joe. The task force operates out of the Medina County Sheriff's Office in Medina and is managed by the DEA's office in Youngstown. But that's not the special part."

"OK, I'll bite. What's the special part?"

"Your role."

"Which would be?"

"For the past year or so, the DEA has been receiving credible reports of theft and corruption within the task force. This covers everything from drugs being stolen from the traffickers and then sold back to them, to money being pocketed during drug busts, to large bribery payments from pill-pushing doctors and pharmacies. But, so far, they've been unable to definitively identify the guilty task force member or members, much less gather sufficient proof."

"Man, that sucks. Not much I hate more than dirty cops."

"I know that. That's one of the reasons we like you for this assignment, Joe. Along with your experience and skills. This would be a rather unusual undercover scenario. You'd be you — no need for a fake cover. But your primary objective while serving as a member of the task force would be to identify the guilty folks and gather enough evidence for their convictions."

"Would this be a full-time or part-time assignment? And for how long? What about Ginny and me being partners?"

"Full-time. It would start next week with a five-day orientation program that the DEA's running in Cincinnati for new task force members throughout Ohio. You'd stay at a hotel in Cincinnati for the course. Then you'd become a full-time member of the task force. You'd get home most weekends, and, depending on what the task force is doing, you might have an occasional weeknight at home. The task force would pay for your hotel room or small apartment in or near Medina. The best guess is that this would be about an eight-month assignment, but it could be shorter or longer depending on how quickly you identify the scumbags. I'd temporarily hook Ginny up with one of the other guys, making it clear that you and she will return to being partners when you get back."

"Wow. Can I have a little time to think this through and discuss it with Ginny before I give you an answer?"

"Sure, but we're on a tight schedule. If you say no, they need to recruit someone else and get them on board in time for that orientation course next week. How about by first thing Wednesday?"

"OK. And do I really have the option of saying 'No thank you' if that's what I decide?"

"Yes, you do. We'd be disappointed, of course. But you could just stay here as you are now with no negative repercussions."

"Good to know. By the way, just out of curiosity, how big is this task force?"

"It's got about 25 full-time members, mostly uniformed and detective personnel from the various cities and towns, plus deputies from a few sheriff's departments. Also a few full-time state folks from the Bureau of Investigation and from the Highway Patrol. And a handful of part-time feds from the FBI, DEA and ATF."

"Man, sounds complicated enough to ensure a whole bunch of bureaucracy, screwed-up communications and backbiting."

"Only three people will know about your undercover assignment — Pete Singleton, the resident agent in charge of the DEA's office in Youngstown, Ginny and me. Everyone else on the task force — and in the department here — will just know you've been temporarily assigned to the task force to put some traffickers away."

"So, I'll be a snitch."

"Call it whatever you want, Joe. We both agree these

crooks ought to be taken down. Like you, I believe a dirty cop is twice as bad as a civilian criminal. Oh, and one other thing. Singleton and I will try our best to have this whole assignment wrap up without anyone else ever knowing it was you who blew the whistle on the bad guys. That may prove to be impossible, but we'll do our best to have it turn out that way."

"And if it doesn't, you and I know how popular I'll be. If I'm lucky, I'll only suffer cops accidentally spilling hot coffee on me. Repeatedly. We know how cops love internal rats." Joe sighed, running a hand through his hair. "OK, not much more to talk about for now. Let me think about it and see what Ginny thinks. I'll get back to you by Wednesday morning."

"Great. Why don't you and Ginny sneak out a little early today? Like now. You've got a lot to talk about."

"Will do."

Chapter 3

Joe took the chief's suggestion. He and Ginny left ten minutes later. While waiting for their Chinese takeout order on their way home, Joe gave Ginny the bare essence of his discussion with the chief. They agreed to get into the heavy discussion after dinner.

They were soon sitting in Joe's kitchen, eating their wonton soup, egg rolls and chicken lo mein with rice. Two beers each rounded out the dinner.

"Before I forget to mention it, Joe, my calls to the taxi company were a bust. Only one of the companies had a pick-up from the school on Saturday. I was all excited until I learned that their customer was a sixty-year-old woman who worked in the school kitchen. Clearly not someone to be confused with Amy."

"Too bad, but it was worth a try. OK, Ginny, let me give you a more detailed replay of my discussion with the chief. And let's not look at our fortune cookies until our discussion is done. We may need them to help us decide which way to go."

Then, as best as he could, Joe gave Ginny an almost verbatim repeat of his discussion in the chief's office. Several times, Ginny was on the verge of interrupting with a question or comment, but she was able to contain herself so that Joe got all the way through without interruption.

"Wow! Is that something you might want? What're your initial thoughts?"

"Total confusion."

"Understood. OK, let's try to organize our thoughts a bit. First, let's list the positive things about this. Then we'll switch to the negatives. I'll take notes."

"OK. Here's how I see the positives. Help put dirty cops away. It's only temporary, not a multi-year assignment. And I don't need a fake identity."

"All good points. Also, the chief said they'd try to arrange things so that your role in this never comes out. Even if it does, cops may be pissed at you, but you're unlikely to be killed — like if you were found out to be undercover in a drug cartel."

"That's a comforting thought, Ginny. Also, the chief said you and I'd be back as partners once this ends."

"That's a biggie for me, Joe. Any other positives?"

"Can't think of any for now. But we may come up with others later or tomorrow. Ready to switch to the negatives?"

"Sure."

"Here goes. I hate snitches, and I'll become one if I say yes. If word gets out, as a minimum, I'll get the cold shoulder from cops for the rest of my career. And I'll have to put up with all the BS and politics of the task force even if my primary objective is this undercover thing."

"This also will put a hold on our house hunting, not to mention our marriage plans."

"True. But in any event, I think we ought to put your condo up for sale now. You're almost never there, so we're just peeing away the money."

"I agree. In fact, we've been in agreement on that for months now. We just have to get off our butts and do it."

"The worst part for me, Ginny, is that, although I'd get home almost all weekends, I'd only rarely — if ever — get home during the week."

"That's a bummer. I've gotten used to your big, manly body cuddled up next to me every night."

"Me too. But it's like a three-hour drive between here and Medina. Each way."

"Yeah, I agree. That's not daily commuting time. Damn."

"How about double damn?"

"Works for me. But back to our list. Anything else?"

"Don't think so. Let me see it," said Joe as he reached across the counter to the pad Ginny was using and spun it around to face him. "OK, we have a nice list. Now what?"

"I say we stop for now. Tomorrow we'll see if we have anything else to add to the list, and then we'll have to weigh the factors and decide. Joe, I just want to make it totally clear that this is your decision in the end, and I'll be one-hundred percent on board with whatever you decide."

"But this choice affects you too, Ginny."

"I know it does, but it affects you more."

"OK. One more important step tonight."

"Oh, what's that?"

"We need to read what our fortune cookies tell us to do."

"Oh, yeah, I forgot." Ginny grabbed the two fortune cookies and gave one to Joe. They each crumbled their cookie and took out the skinny strip of paper.

"You first, Ginny."

Ginny straightened out her strip of paper and read, "'Luck is 50% perspiration plus 50% inspiration.' Nice, but not exactly a fortune. And surely not much help with your task force decision. If anything, it probably relates more to our solving cases here. What does yours say?"

"'You have rice stuck between your teeth.' Just kidding. It really says, 'Do not fear what you don't know.'"

"Well, that sorta says don't fear the task force option, but it's not exactly a fortune either."

"I think too many lawyers have gotten involved with fortune cookies. Afraid of being sued if they predict something and it doesn't come true. Can't the lawyers leave anything alone?"

"OK, Joe. Enough of this. Let's watch a dumb TV show to turn our brains off and then head to bed."

"That's the kind of fortune I can agree with."

Chapter 4

Despite their expectations, Ginny and Joe both slept soundly. They were back at their desks by eight the next morning.

On Ginny's desk was a fax. "Joe, Franley kept her word. This fax from her came in yesterday, after we had left. It's the dates of Amy's runaways since she started at Pond View. And it does look like two or three a year."

"Good for Franley."

"It'll be tough to keep our minds off our big upcoming decision, but we do need to focus on our missing student. Needless to say, she hasn't yet returned to school. And I assume no one's heard from her or they'd have notified us."

"Agreed. We oughta go back to the school and meet with some of her friends and classmates. Somebody might have seen her leaving. Or might know something. I can't believe that canvassing the neighborhood and checking nearby camera recordings came up with nothing. She didn't just disappear into thin air. A girl who's run off as often as she has must have left some kind of trail."

"Let's swing by the crime scene guys on the way out and see if they found anything of interest in her dorm room last evening."

"OK. Oh, and while you were down the hall, the sergeant called. Fortunately, searching that pond area didn't turn up her body. And, by the way, he asked me to thank you for the easy search you requested. He said the pond is small and was still fully frozen, so searching it and the 10- or 12-acre surrounding woods took next to no time."

"I guess he owes me one. Let's head on out. And, Joe, when we're done, I'd like to talk with her parents again. Any friends other than classmates? Like from the neighborhood. Was she especially close to any of her teachers or someone in the administration? How much money does she normally have or have access to, and where does she get cash? They must have some ideas about where she goes when she runs off. I can't help but believe someone knows more than they've told us."

"Looks like we've got a good part of the day laid out for us. Perhaps we should sneak out early again today. One way or the other, I need to give the chief my answer by tomorrow morning. And, although very objective, flipping a coin probably isn't the best way to make a decision like this."

After quick stops in the restrooms and then to fill their coffee containers, Joe and Ginny walked down the stairs to the crime scene guys. The report was very short and clear: The techs found absolutely nothing of interest.

A few minutes later, Joe and Ginny were in Ginny's car on the way to Pond View. When they arrived, they entered the administration building and walked up to the same receptionist they'd met the day before. She recognized them and, as they requested, immediately escorted them to the office of Mrs. Porter, the dean of students.

"Good morning."

"Good morning, Detectives. Any news?"

"No, nothing yet. We'd like to speak with some of Amy's friends and classmates. There's a good possibility that someone saw or heard something. Or knows something about her prior runaways."

"Sure, happy to oblige. Normally we'd be concerned about word getting out and some of the girls getting upset or scared, but we're past that. Word has spread like a raging wildfire. In fact, your speaking with some of the students might put their minds at ease a bit. Let's head over to the dining room. We should be able to catch a bunch of the girls still having breakfast."

Porter grabbed her coat and led the two detectives outside to another large building a couple of hundred feet away. She led them through the front doors into a large foyer, and then through a wide set of double doors into the dining room. There were close to 40 tables in the room, each able to accommodate two, four or eight people. About one-third of the seats were occupied. Porter led Joe and Ginny to the front of the large room and loudly clapped her hands to get everyone's attention. The buzz of conversations quickly came to a halt.

"Girls. Girls. Your attention please. I'm sure you are all aware that one of your classmates, Amy Richardson, has been missing since sometime Saturday. Here with me are Detectives Harris and McFarland from the Jasper Creek Police Department. They're trying to find Amy. They have a few things to say to you, and we're hoping that one or more of you knows or saw something that can help with the search. This is important, so please pay attention. It shouldn't take too long, but don't worry if it makes some of you late for first period. I'll send a message to all the teachers explaining the reason for your possible lateness."

Ginny then took a step forward and gave a brief

summary of what they knew about Amy's disappearance. "My partner, Detective McFarland, and I will now circulate around the room, spending a few minutes at each table. If you know anything, no matter how insignificant it may seem, please tell us. If you'd like to speak with us privately, that won't be a problem — just let us know and we'll arrange it. And thank you for your cooperation."

Ginny and Joe started at opposite ends of the room, spending a few minutes sitting at each table with students at it. Almost all the girls appeared to be sincere in trying to help, but they didn't seem to know much that Ginny and Joe didn't already know.

Back in Ginny's car ninety minutes later, she and Joe sat in front of the administration building sharing their notes. They had picked up a number of details, but nothing that seemed to provide a big lead forward. Amy often bragged about how easy it was to sneak away, and that the school couldn't do anything about it. Amy always seemed to have a lot of cash, perhaps a few hundred dollars. She had an ATM card and was able to get cash whenever she wanted from the ATM in the student lounge. Amy often said that her parents didn't care about her — they were totally into themselves. As long as Amy didn't cause them problems or require them to alter their schedules, she could do whatever she wanted.

"So what we learned, Ginny, is that she is indeed a spoiled brat. And a rich one at that."

"True. We also learned that she most likely had enough cash for buses or taxis or trains. And for meals and a hotel, without having to use a credit card."

"It's not much, but it's more than we knew before we got here."

"True enough. OK, ready to head to her parents?"

"Sure. Let's go for it. We should see if her parents have the bank statements showing all of Amy's withdrawals from the ATM at school. We can then check if large withdrawals correlate with the dates of her runaways."

"Good idea."

Ginny drove to Avon, and the two detectives were soon once again sitting with Mrs. Richardson in the sunroom.

"Mr. Richardson will be sorry he missed you. He left early this morning on a business trip to Chicago. He'll be back Friday night."

"Yes, well, it's our fault," said Ginny. "We dropped in without making an appointment first. But you should be able to help us. We can see Mr. Richardson at a later date if it proves necessary."

"What have you learned so far?"

"Not too much yet," said Joe. "But it does continue to look likely that she left voluntarily, without being forced to. Our crime scene techs were at the school last evening. They thoroughly examined her room and found nothing suspicious."

"Mrs. Richardson," said Ginny, "do you have a recent photo of Amy? We'd like to include it in a statewide BOLO, that's a 'Be on the lookout' alert'. We want to also list her in NamUs."

"NamUs?"

"Sorry for the jargon. NamUs is the National Missing and Unidentified Persons System. Her description will be visible nationwide. We doubt that we need to go national, but that's the most effective way to get her description to all the local surrounding states."

"Mrs. Richardson, can you give us any additional identification details for Amy? Any scars or tattoos? Anything else that could help someone identify her?"

Richardson excused herself for a few minutes, came back and gave Ginny a half-dozen photos of Amy. As she'd told the detectives the previous day, she reiterated that Amy was five-foot-six, about 145 pounds, and had no scars or tattoos. Light brown hair and blue-gray eyes.

Mrs. Richardson indicated that they knew Amy had been dating last year and earlier this year, but they didn't know any names or whether it was one or several different boys. "You know how private and noncommunicative girls of her age are. Especially with their parents."

"Who are her closest friends at school?" asked Joe. "Is she particularly close to any of the teachers or administrative staff?"

"As I said, Amy is pretty private, especially with us. But, obviously, one of her best friends is her roommate, Carol Davis. This is the third year they're rooming together. She also speaks highly of Miss or Mrs. Kendall, the woman in charge of her dorm. And she's always talking about how wonderful one of her teachers is. What's his name again? Darn, I wish my husband were here. He'd remember his name in a second. Let me think. Um, Newburg. No, Newman. That's it, Newman. He was Amy's chemistry teacher last year. Amy is always saying how wonderful a teacher and how caring he is. To the point that my husband told me that he thinks Amy has some child-like crush on him."

"Thank you, Mrs. Richardson," said Joe. "We'd also like to see your bank statements. For whichever account is tied to Amy's credit card."

"OK. But why?"

"We want to compare her charges and ATM withdrawals with the dates of all the times she's run off. May show nothing, but it could be useful."

"Hold on. Let me go dig them out. Anything that might help."

Richardson left the detectives but returned a few minutes later. "Here're the statements," she said as she handed a file to Joe. "Fortunately, my husband saves everything. Forever."

"Thank you. We'll make a copy of what we need and get these back to you in the next day or two."

"That'll be fine. There's no rush."

"Mrs. Richardson," said Ginny, "unless something develops between now and then, we think it would be a good idea for you and Mr. Richardson to hold a brief press conference Thursday evening. Our press office can arrange all the details."

"A press conference?"

"Yes," said Joe. "The idea would be for you and your husband to speak to your daughter, through the camera, telling her to come back home — or at least contact you. Tell her you love her and are worried about her. Then, also add if someone is holding her without her consent they should please not hurt her, but instead contact you and say what they want. You'll do whatever is necessary to get Amy safely back home. Finally, describe Amy and ask anyone who may have seen her to call us at the phone number showing on their TV screen."

"I understand. I've seen several of those on TV over the years. But, as I told you, my husband is out of town until Friday night."

"Yes," said Joe, "but I assume he'll change his schedule for something like this."

"That's pretty unlikely. His business trips are import-ant. And surely not worth messing with for something that Amy almost certainly brought on herself."

"Well, that's up to you and your husband," said Ginny. "If Mr. Richardson isn't back, can you handle the press conference by yourself?"

"Um, I guess so. If I have to, I have to."

Before they left, Joe and Ginny got Amy's cellphone and credit card numbers.

"OK then," said Ginny, "we'll let you know if anything new develops. You should hear from our press folks sometime Thursday morning. And, if not sooner, we'll see you Thursday evening at the press conference. If this follows the normal procedure, it'll probably be timed to make the six-o'clock news live. And probably take place in your driveway to maximize the emotional impact on viewers."

Driving back to their office, they agreed that while Ginny would issue the BOLO and enter Amy's data into NamUs, Joe would have one of the techs request a check by the phone company of text messages and voicemail messages left on Amy's phone as well as an alert if her credit card was used.

"Wow!" said Ginny. "I can't believe her own father won't modify his all-important business trip for this. Hell, I'm surprised he went at all while his daughter's missing."

"The parents seem to care a lot more about themselves than their daughter. I'm not a shrink, but I sure can see a link between that and Amy's many runaways."

"Yup. Either they don't care or they're totally convinced, and pissed, that this is just Amy running off once again."

"Could be either."

"Ginny, we also should get back to the school and talk with that chemistry teacher. We've already spoken with her roommate and dorm director, but not with him. You never know."

"Definitely. Can't hurt."

Back in the PD parking lot, Joe and Ginny decided to walk around the corner to their frequent lunch spot, Sancho's Taco Shop. As it was already close to 2:00 PM, Sancho's was almost empty. Joe and Ginny had no problem having private discussions about Amy's disappearance and their upcoming decision deadline regarding the drug task force while simultaneously munching on two soft tacos each.

When they returned to their desks, Ginny got right to work on the BOLO and NamUS while Joe did the same with regard to Amy's cellphone and credit card. They filled the chief in on their day and Joe committed to being back first thing in the morning with a decision about the drug task force. They told the chief they were heading out early again, and they were out of the parking lot and on their way to Joe's house by four o'clock. Before they left, they called Sergeant Watkins in the press office, filled him in on the case and explained the need for him to arrange the Thursday evening press conference.

Chapter 5

Having had a late lunch, neither of the detectives was ready for a large dinner. Ginny poured a jar of salsa in a bowl, opened a large bag of tortillas and put it on the kitchen counter. Joe grabbed a cold six-pack from the refrigerator and dinner was served.

Ginny jumped right in. "OK, Joe. No thinking. Your immediate reaction? Yes or no to the task force?"

"Umm. Yes. I guess."

"Not surprised. That's where I thought you'd wind up."

"Yeah, but it's not all one-sided. I have a lot of reservations and concerns."

"I'm sure you do. And you should. You'd also have a bunch if you decided no."

"That's true."

"OK, Joe. Let's talk it out. Maybe we can eliminate a few of your concerns, or at least come up with a way to deal with some of them."

"This could be a late night."

"Not a problem. This is important. Let's give it whatever time it needs tonight."

"OK. Here's number one. The toughest part will be us not working together every day. I'll miss us not being on the same cases."

"Me too. It's also a bummer that you won't be home

every night. At least you'll be home weekends. I know — maybe not every weekend, but most. And we'll be able to talk most nights. We can tell each other what we're working on, what the problems are, what we're planning next, and so on."

"True. We can at least be a sounding board for each other. It'll sorta feel like we're working the cases together."

"That's the hope. What's your next concern, Joe?"

"I hate that this puts a real wrench in the timing of our getting married."

"Yeah, well, it's not like we've picked a date and invited everyone and now we have to change everything."

"Agreed. But, as a minimum, I really do think we've got to get off our butts and put your condo on the market. We're wasting money every month we delay, plus who knows how long it'll take to sell."

"Deal. We both agree on that. Tell you what. I'll do a thorough cleaning of the condo early next week, then meet with a few realtors. I can do it in the evenings while you're away at the orientation. I'll arrange for them to come back next Saturday and make their pitches to us. You know, how much the condo is worth, how quickly they can sell it and, of course, why they're better than all the other realtors. We'll then pick one and get on with it."

"Sounds good to me."

"OK if I add one of my reservations, Joe?"

"Sure. This is a team sport."

"I'll be worried sick about you. Even though your main objective is to identify the dirty task force members, you'll be working the drug scene and dealing with the worst of the worst every day. Besides promising to be careful, which I know you will be, you need to promise to call or text me at least once a day, even if it just says 'hi.'"

"No problem with that. But don't worry, I'll be super careful. Ginny, I've got one more reservation."

"Which is?"

"I fully understand the importance of identifying the dirty agents, and as much as I can't think of anyone worse than a dirty cop, I still feel bad about being a rat. I know it's illogical, but it is what it is."

"I understand that. But I think you'll feel good when you put them away. Even if your role can't be kept secret and cops everywhere hate you, you and I will know that you did the right thing. And most cops, down deep even if they won't admit it, will feel the same way."

"I hear you. Intellectually, I know you're right, but my gut hasn't yet fully realized it. It probably needs a bit more time."

"Believe me, I understand exactly what you're feeling. But there's probably nothing we can do besides letting time do its thing."

"Agreed."

"OK, anything else?"

"No, I don't think so. The one good thing is that it won't last forever and will hopefully be over in eight months. Maybe even sooner."

"Yeah, knowing that can help us put up with most anything — for a temporary period."

"OK, that's it now. Looks like I'm about to become a task force member. I'll let the chief know first thing in the morning. How about we head off to bed now and take care of some other important business?"

"Works for me. But I'm pretty sure you're thinking of monkey business."

"I'll just plead the fifth on that," said Joe with a grin as he and Ginny got up and headed for the bedroom.

Chapter 6

Joe and Ginny got to the station about 7:30 the next morning. Joe was at the chief's doorway right after the chief arrived a few minutes before eight. Joe followed him in and closed the office door.

"OK, Chief, as promised, I made the big decision."

"And?"

"I'm in."

"Glad to hear that, Joe," said the chief as he stood up, reached across his desk and shook Joe's hand. "I'm sure it wasn't an easy call for you. Or for Ginny. But you're the right person for the assignment, and I'm pretty sure you'll start feeling a lot better about it once you begin to achieve some results."

"Sure hope so."

"OK, let me call Resident Agent in Charge Singleton and give him the good news. I'm sure he or one of his staff will be in touch with the details for next week's orientation. And at some point, Singleton will want to meet you and, of course, discuss the details of your assignment."

"OK, I'll wait to hear from somebody. In any event, thanks for the vote of confidence, Chief."

"Well deserved, Joe. Now see if you and Ginny can make some progress on that missing schoolgirl case while you're still here."

"Will do." Before leaving the chief's office, Joe got the

chief to agree to extra staffing and overtime for several of the detectives for phone coverage after Mrs. Richardson's upcoming press conference.

Back at his desk, Joe quietly filled Ginny in on his discussion with the chief. They then spoke to everyone in the room and arranged for seven detectives to put in extra hours between Thursday and Saturday nights to answer the barrage of calls expected after Thursday's press conference.

Joe then checked whether anything useful came from researching Amy's cellphone data.

"Sorry, Joe, but we got nothing. The phone has been turned off since Saturday morning. No chance of checking her recent whereabouts. We checked the texts and voicemail messages on her phone, but nothing unusual popped up. Short messages and texts with a few classmates and her mother, and a few texts to restaurants that deliver. That's it."

"OK, appreciate your trying. Guess she turned the phone off to avoid us tracking her. Or her abductor, if there is one, did."

"No way for us to tell who turned it off."

"I know. Just talking out loud to myself. Again, thanks anyhow."

"Don't mention it."

Joe reported his discussion about Amy's phone to Ginny.

"Joe, what's your impression — runaway or abduction?"

"I'm still leaning towards runaway. I think the parents would have heard something by now if there was a kidnapper. It'll be four full days after lunch today. I hope I'm right. Otherwise she was abducted, but not for ransom. It's either to kill her or enslave her, maybe sell her off."

"Jeez. Let's hope it is just a teenage runaway. Or, it still might be a kidnapping. What if the kidnappers did contact her parents, but they're keeping it quiet? Hell, maybe the father's in Chicago to raise the ransom money."

"Possible. But I don't think so. I don't think the mother could be such a good actress knowing that her daughter, an only child no less, was kidnapped. They didn't seem very worried or scared, just mad at their daughter for running off. Again."

"Yeah, you're probably right, Joe. But what say we take another shot at the mother and see if we can break her composure?"

"Works for me. Let's go."

"Give me a few minutes. I want to copy the bank statements Mrs. Richardson gave us. Then we can give her back the originals."

Joe pulled up and parked in the Richardsons' driveway about an hour later.

"Oh, hello, Detectives. Do you have some news? Please, please, tell me Amy is OK."

"Sorry, Mrs. Richardson," said Ginny, "we don't have any news yet."

"Oh," said Mrs. Richardson, as she led the detectives into the living room and sat down, or rather collapsed, into the first chair she came to.

Joe and Ginny sat on a couch facing her.

Ginny returned the bank statements to Mrs. Richardson. "Thank you."

"Were they helpful?"

"We haven't yet had a chance to analyze them," said Ginny. "We just made copies so that we could return the originals."

"Oh. Thank you."

"We actually stopped by to try and learn a little more about Amy," said Joe. "Any unusual activities or moods in the days before she went missing? Any new friends? Or boyfriends? How was her relationship with you? And with your husband? Any little detail you can think of might prove to be helpful in our investigation."

They spent about twenty-five minutes talking, mostly Joe and Ginny pulling bits of information from Mrs. Richardson.

"OK, that's it for now," said Ginny.

"I hope I was of some help. I'm really worried about Amy now. She's never stayed away this long before."

"We understand," said Ginny. "We're doing everything we can."

"I know."

"Mrs. Richardson," said Joe, "if we don't speak again beforehand, we'll see you tomorrow evening back here for the press conference. We'll be sure to get here well before it starts."

Back in the car, Ginny said, "Well, that wasn't very useful. She didn't tell us anything new that's helpful. On the other hand, it did further convince me that she's telling us all that she knows."

"I agree. But it is amazing. I mean, I'm sure most girls Amy's age don't fully confide in their parents like they did when they were younger. But these folks and their daughter are almost strangers. At least the mother seems to care. The father's off on a business trip like he's got no cares in the world. I don't get it."

"You and I are on the same page. But I'm glad we did this. I'm pretty sure at this point that they've not heard from any kidnapper."

"Yup. And luckily, Ginny, it's almost noon so we'll be just on time for lunch at Sancho's."

"Lucky us."

Ginny and Joe were back at their desks about ninety minutes later, following their normal Tex-Mex lunch.

Joe had a message that RAC Singleton had called. Joe called him back. Singleton welcomed Joe to the task force and expressed his pleasure that Joe had accepted the undercover assignment. Singleton said his assistant would send all the details of the orientation course by overnight delivery. He also indicated his desire to meet with Joe early the following week before he fully jumped into his new assignment.

Joe walked down the hall and filled the chief in.

"Glad to hear it. You'll like Singleton. Seems to be a straight-up guy. Now, I think it's time to tell everyone about your new assignment. Why don't you go get Ginny so the three of us can go over everything first?"

"Will do."

Joe went back to his desk, told Ginny that the chief wanted to speak with both of them, and followed Ginny into the chief's office, closing the door behind himself.

"Ginny, I just told Joe that I want to announce his task force assignment now. It starts next week, and I don't want people to learn about it second or third-hand. Plus, we need to arrange and announce your new temporary partner until Joe's return, or at least until this missing-girl situation is solved."

"Chief, who're you planning to team me up with?"

"I've been thinking Caruso. I think he and you would complement each other well. You're more analytical and thoughtful, whereas he tends to be more intuitive. The combination of your approaches should be synergistic, as they say. Plus, you and he seem to get along pretty well together."

"Working with Denny would be fine."

"OK, then. Let's head out and make the big announcement. As I said, I'm not sure whether you and Caruso will partner until Joe returns, or just for this case. We'll see how things work out."

"Got it."

The chief led them out of his office, where he stood and bellowed for everyone to gather around for a quick announcement. As Joe watched everyone approach, he was sure that several of them were expecting the chief to announce Joe was leaving the department, either voluntarily or forced. *Won't they be surprised!*

"A couple of things. First, I'm pleased to announce that Joe has been offered and has accepted a temporary assignment to a DEA drug task force. This assignment is expected to last somewhere between six and twelve months. While it lasts, it will be a full-time assignment. The task force covers the northeast part of the state. It operates out of Medina. Joe starts on Monday with a one-week DEA-led orientation course for new task force members. I'm sure you'll all join me in congratulating Joe on being selected for this."

A few minutes of clapping, smiles and teasing comments from the gathered group followed.

"Secondly, and of course, related, Ginny is going to team up with Caruso on the missing schoolgirl case she and Joe have been working. Not sure if this partnership will be just for this case or until Joe returns. We'll see. OK, that's it. Let's get back to catching bad guys." With that, the chief turned and was back in his office before anyone could say or ask anything.

A few comments were made to Joe, to Ginny and to Caruso; everyone was soon back at their desks. Except for Caruso, who followed Joe and Ginny back to theirs.

"Joe, seriously. We were teasing you, but we're all impressed. Congratulations on being picked. And kudos for being willing to do it. I'm sure it'll take a lot of extra time and effort."

"Thanks, Denny."

"And, Ginny, I'm delighted to be working with you."

"Same here. By the way, we've arranged for the missing girl's mother to hold a press conference tomorrow evening. You ought to be there. And the three of us should spend some time tomorrow getting you up to speed on the case."

"Sounds like a plan."

Joe and Ginny brought their notes up to date and left around 4:30. Caruso spent his time organizing his current cases, knowing that some of them would be handed off to other detectives so that he could focus with Ginny on the Richardson case.

Chapter 7

Thursday morning, Ginny and Joe spent about an hour with Caruso, filling him in on everything they had done and learned since the 9-1-1 call on Monday that led to the chief assigning them the case.

"Denny, Joe and I have intentionally not told you our thoughts about the case. You should go through this — unfortunately — thin case file first." Handing the file to Caruso, Ginny continued, "After that, we can discuss whether we, and you, think this was a runaway or a kidnapping or a snatch for some other reason, whether we believe and/or blame one or both of the parents, and so on. You should begin to form your own opinions before we contaminate your thinking with what we think."

"Fair enough. How about we do that over lunch? Perhaps at Golden Sun, if you guys are willing to forgo your daily Mexican ritual for some good Chinese food."

"Deal," said Joe. "Hell, an egg roll is just a different type of burrito shell with a slightly different filling." Everyone chuckled and agreed to head for lunch at 11:30 to beat any noontime crowd.

Joe and Ginny happily accepted Caruso's offer to try to correlate Amy's credit card charges and ATM withdrawals with her runaway dates. Ginny gave Caruso the copies of the bank statements.

Just before eleven, Joe received the promised overnight

envelope from the DEA office in Youngstown. In it, Joe found the detailed schedule of the orientation program, brief biographies of the instructors and attendees and all the logistical details he needed to know: the name and address of the hotel where a reservation had been made for him, along with the name and contact information of his assigned roommate; the dress code (so-called "business casual"); meal times; the times that sessions and breaks started and ended; information about laundry machines and nearby shops; the no-smoking and no-alcohol policies; and so on. There was also a handful of documents about drugs, the DEA, and drug task forces that Joe would have to read, or at least browse through, over the weekend. Joe was glad to see how organized the DEA, or at least Singleton, seemed to be. Maybe it boded well for the task force. Joe also decided that, when he had a few minutes, he'd call his roommate-to-be, just to say hello. Joe couldn't remember the last time he had a roommate other than Ginny, and before her his now-deceased wife.

The three detectives left PD headquarters at exactly 11:30 and were seated with menus in hand at the Golden Sun restaurant by 11:50. All three went with the daily lunch special, along with hot tea.

An hour later they were ready to leave the restaurant, their stomachs full, the bill paid and the Amy Richardson case having been thoroughly discussed. Caruso agreed with Joe and Ginny that Amy running away was the most likely scenario, but that her running away was beginning to look less certain as more time passed. With her disappearance having occurred five days earlier, no contact from a kidnapper made kidnapping increasingly unlikely. If she was taken, it more likely was for any of a number of unseemly reasons — murder, sex slavery or child pornography, sale of a child, and so on.

As Caruso hadn't met Amy's parents, until he could form his own opinion, he accepted Joe and Ginny's belief that, although they certainly had some flaws as parents, they didn't seem to be involved in — or holding back information about — their daughter's disappearance.

Walking back from lunch, Ginny laid out the details for the planned press conference that evening. "It's scheduled to start at six. Expect to have all the local papers and TV there. Also, a few from Dayton and Columbus. I'll say a few opening comments, and then turn it over to Mrs. Richardson. I still can't believe her husband isn't coming back from Chicago for this. Hell, I can't believe he went to Chicago in the first place. We ought to plan on getting to her house by five. I want to review what she's going to say with her. Plus, I'm sure it'll help her to see a few familiar faces there."

"And, Denny, we want to make the transition from me to you as smooth as possible. I don't want any change to spook her, or for her to spend time trying to analyze what important conclusions to reach from my handoff to you."

"Understood."

"OK," said Ginny, "let's plan on leaving here at 4:30. I assume you'll follow Joe and me in your car. That way we can all head home directly from there when it's over."

"I'll be ready."

Once back at his desk, Joe called Corporal Vegas of the State Highway Patrol.

"Vegas. Highway Patrol."

"Hello, Corporal. This is Detective Joe McFarland. With the Jasper Creek PD."

"Yes, how can I help you? Do we know each other?"

"No, not yet. But we will soon."

"Huh?"

"We're both attending the drug task force orientation program next week in Cincinnati, and we're assigned as roommates in the nearby Hampton Inn."

"Oh, I didn't know. Sorry. Nice to meet you."

"Guess you didn't look at the material they sent out to all of us."

"No, not yet. I was told that an express envelope arrived for me this morning, but I haven't seen it yet. I'm a supervisor out here on the highways around Toledo, and I'll only be back at the barracks at end of shift."

"Well, I just wanted to say hello. Break the ice sort of, before we meet up on Monday."

"Great idea. Glad you did it. Where you gonna be working once the orientation is over?"

"On a task force in the northeast part of the state. You?"

"Mine's mostly a highway-related task force. Pretty much running through the middle of the state, from Columbus east to the West Virginia state line. Seems like a lot of drugs are following that route."

"Interesting. Well, I'll let you get back to work. As I said, just wanted to break the ice."

"Appreciate you taking the initiative, Joe. See you Monday."

"Yup. Have a good one."

Ginny spent about an hour calling three realtors and

arranging for them to meet her at her condo during the next week, one each on Tuesday, Wednesday and Thursday evening. That would give Ginny time to clean and straighten up on Monday evening. She also scheduled the three realtors with separate times to come back a week from Saturday and meet with Joe and her.

Mid-afternoon, Caruso rolled up a chair next to Ginny's desk and spoke with Ginny and Joe. "The good news is that I went through all of Amy's credit card charges and withdrawals. The bad news is I got nada."

"Nada?" asked Joe.

"Yup. Her charges were totally innocuous. Mostly nearby restaurants and fast-food places. A few ladies' clothing stores and the school bookstore and snack bar. That was it."

"And the cash withdrawals?" asked Ginny.

"There were quite a few. No established pattern. Typically a withdrawal every six or seven weeks. Usually for $200. No change in pattern related to any of her runaways, except there was never a withdrawal during any of the dates she was actually missing."

"Good work, Denny," said Joe. "Too bad. I was hoping to see a large withdrawal just before each incident."

"Yeah, I know. Would have been a good indication that all the runaways, including this one, were voluntary and premeditated. Sorry, but it is what it is."

"For sure," said Ginny. "Thanks for doing the checking. At least we've now eliminated one place we need to further investigate."

Chapter 8

Before they knew it, it was 4:30. Joe and Ginny were in Joe's car, with Caruso following them in his. They were ringing the Richardsons' doorbell slightly before five. Mrs. Richardson put her coat on and joined the detectives outside, and she and Caruso were introduced to each other. They all watched as the TV cameramen set up their equipment, with a grouping of all their microphones in front of a podium that had been placed where the driveway and the front walk intersected. A few of the TV and newspaper reporters were already on hand, gathered around a food truck from which they all seemed to have purchased cups of smoking, hot coffee.

"Oh, my God," said Mrs. Richardson, "there are so many reporters here."

"Yes, there are," said Ginny. "And there'll be several more by the time we start."

"Probably also a news helicopter or two," said Joe.

Ginny explained how Joe had been assigned to a special statewide project that would take up much of his time, and that Detective Caruso was assigned to this case so there'd be no break in their efforts to find and return Amy. Richardson seemed to understand and accept the change.

"Let's just walk through the press conference itself," said Ginny. "At exactly six o'clock, I'll make some brief introductory comments, and then introduce you. You should plan on speaking for about five minutes, give or take. Something along the lines of 'Amy, if you're watching this, please know that your father and I love you very much and are worried about you. If you can call or come home, please do it. We're not mad at you. We just want you to be safely back here. And if there's someone or someones who abducted Amy, please don't hurt her. She's done nothing to deserve this. Let us know what you want. We'll do anything we possibly can to get Amy safely back home. And if anyone knows or saw something that might be relevant, please call the Jasper Creek Police Department. Thank you.'"

"OK."

"I'll then get back up and say a few final things, like we can be reached by calling the number shown on the screen. We'll then take a few questions, and that will be it."

"You make it sound so easy. I'm scared to death."

"I can imagine," said Joe. "But I think once it gets underway and you start talking, your nervousness will go away."

"I sure hope so."

They went back into the house for a few minutes to use the restrooms and have some water, and for the women to freshen up their makeup.

The doorbell rang around 5:45, and in walked the chief. Joe, Ginny and Caruso were surprised; the chief had given no indication that he'd be attending.

"Chief, surprised to see you here," said Joe. "You didn't say anything earlier. What changed your mind?"

"Just a little thing called the mayor. He felt it important to show the focus we're putting on this case. And no, I didn't tell him we thought that Amy had voluntarily run away."

"No surprise there."

"So I'll take three or four minutes to kick the press conference off, and then I'll turn it over to you guys. I'll just stand there on the side, trying to look important. Which of you should I turn it over to?"

"That'll be me," said Ginny. "I'll say a little bit and then introduce Mrs. Richardson. Then I'll wrap it up at the end."

Just then, Richardson returned from the restroom, and Ginny introduced her and the chief.

"I'm pleased to meet you, ma'am. Too bad it's under these circumstances."

Tearing up and struggling to prevent her tears racing down her cheeks, Richardson replied, "Thank you, Chief. I appreciate your being here."

"Don't mention it. And I want you to know we have some of our best detectives and all our support staff working on this."

"I know that. Thank you."

"OK, let's head on outside. It's almost six," said Ginny.

Despite the frigid weather, the detectives and the chief took their coats off for the press conference. Mrs. Richardson kept her coat on and added a wool scarf around her neck. Five minutes later, the press conference began. There were about a dozen TV and newspaper reporters, plus another dozen or so cameramen and technicians. The press conference went just as expected: the chief, then Ginny, then Richardson and then Ginny again. Ginny managed a short Q & A session at the end. The questions were as inane as could be. "Mrs. Richardson, do you know where your daughter is?" "Mrs. Richardson, what do you think happened to her?" "Detective, do you think kidnapping or murder is more likely?" "Mrs. Richardson, if it's a kidnapping, how much are you willing or able to pay as ransom?" Wisely, Ginny ended the session fairly quickly.

A few "well dones" and "thank yous," and all the police were soon gone. The reporters also left as soon as their equipment was packed up and loaded in their vans or cars. Even the two circling helicopters left the scene.

Back in Joe's car and heading to his house, Ginny said, "Well, I'm glad that's over."

"Understood. But it went well. You did a good job, and even Mrs. Richardson held up well. The one point where she had to stop speaking for a minute to regain her composure actually helped make her seem that much more real."

"I agree. Still hard to believe that her husband left her to handle this all by herself."

"Not sure if it's weird or cold or selfish, but it surely isn't normal."

"I'm with you on that, Joe. But, boy, what a bunch of stupid questions from the reporters."

"Yup, but that's about what you should expect from that crew."

"Well, let's hope it triggers Amy or her abductor or some witnesses to call. 'Cause right now, we're totally out of leads."

"Hang in there, Ginny. We're often out of leads on a case, and then something pops."

"True enough. Either by luck, pure luck. Or our poking causes the luck. Or, like my fortune cookie said the other night — inspiration plus perspiration. OK, enough of this for now. Let's get home, have some dinner and settle in for some stimulating TV."

"Sounds like a plan to me."

Chapter 9

First thing Friday morning, Ginny and Caruso drove to Pond View Academy. Ginny introduced Caruso and Franley to each other and explained how Caruso would be filling in for Joe, who was on a special assignment.

"We'd like to interview a few of Amy's teachers from prior years," said Ginny. "We've already spoken to most from this year. We'd like to specifically interview Mr. Newman, plus perhaps two others."

"Not a problem. Why don't you use the same office as a few days ago? I'll call Ms. LaForte, our academic dean. She can arrange the interviews and cover the classes while each teacher is here with you. I'll ask her to start with Mr. Newman."

"Thank you."

About fifteen minutes later, there was a knock on the door jam of the small office the detectives were using, and Professor Newman walked in."

"Excuse me. I'm Howard Newman. I was told you wanted to speak with me."

"Yes. Please come in and have a seat," said Ginny, who then introduced herself and Caruso.

Newman sat down and asked, "How can I help you?"

"We'd like to talk with you about Amy Richardson. We're trying to find her or find out what's happened to her. Did you happen to see the press conference with her mother yesterday?"

"No. I almost never watch TV, but I read about it in this morning's paper. Terrible. Just terrible. I hope she's all right."

"Mr. Newman," said Caruso, "we know she was in your chemistry class last year. What can you tell us about her?"

"An extremely bright girl. A bit shy in class, but a quick learner. In fact, I was disappointed that she didn't continue with Advanced Chemistry this year. But that was her choice."

"Do you have any idea where she may have gone? Or possibly with who?"

"What? No. Why would you think I might?"

"We understood that the two of you had a rather close relationship. She looked up to you, and we thought she might have mentioned something to you," said Ginny.

"She didn't. Our relationship was totally about chemistry. We never got into personal things."

"We've been told that she continued to periodically come to your office this year even though she wasn't taking any chemistry courses."

"Yes, that's true. It seemed rather unusual to me, but she, in fact, always had chemistry-related questions. Some tough ones, I might add. She often would then try to steer the conversation to her personal life, especially what she considered a very poor relationship with her parents, especially her father. But I always cut those conversations off. I felt that they were none of my business and not appropriate topics for us to discuss."

"Did you ever get the sense that she had a crush on you?" asked Caruso.

"Huh? Definitely not. If there was any kind of such feelings on her part, I surely didn't recognize or encourage it. The only thing I can think of is that she was looking for some kind of father figure who cared about her. To make up for what she believed was her father's lack of interest and love."

"So you have no idea where she may have gone? This time or any of the other times? And possibly with whom?"

"That's correct."

Ginny and Caruso thanked Newman, gave him their cards and asked that he call them if he thought of or heard anything else.

The two detectives then interviewed Mrs. Browning, Amy's English teacher from the prior year, and Mr. Vintor, her math teacher from the prior year. Neither was able to provide any new information.

Ginny and Caruso said good-bye to Franley and left. They were back at their desks a little before noon.

Most of the rest of the day was pretty much a waste. Joe, Ginny and Caruso spent almost all of their time answering calls resulting from the press conference. It seemed that everyone, and their brothers, saw a girl who might be Amy — riding a bus, boarding a train, sitting next to a "big man" driving a car. CNN and some of the other national cable news shows picked up the story, so calls were coming in from all over the country.

Out of all the calls, only five or six seemed to merit any

follow-up. Ginny and Caruso were gone for about two hours, following up the few local calls of interest. Joe remained at his desk, answering new calls. He also contacted the PDs of San Francisco and Albany, New York, for two out-of-town calls he judged worthy of a second look. Both turned out to be worthless.

When Ginny and Caruso returned, Joe was disappointed (but not surprised) to learn that the local calls they'd followed up on had proven to be a waste of time. Joe and Ginny had decided to leave around four. Caruso had arranged for two other detectives and him to come in and cover the phones the next day; Saturday might prove to be a heavy call day.

Around three o'clock, Detectives Klein and Jones walked into the large room. Klein was carrying a big cake box, and Jones had two six-packs of soda cans.

"OK, everyone, gather around," said Klein. "Time for Joe's farewell party."

"We were going to get something nice for you, Joe," said Jones, "but then we remembered you'll be coming back to us. That sure put a damper on our celebration."

Everyone, including Joe, laughed. The chief came out of his office. Everyone enjoyed the cake and soda, while tossing a steady stream of teasing insults at Joe. After about 20 minutes people started walking up to Joe, wishing him the best, either shaking his hand or hugging him, and then returning to their own desks and back to work.

Joe thanked everyone and said his good-byes; he and

Ginny were in his car and on their way home by 4:30. They stopped at the supermarket and picked up what they needed for dinner, and were soon in Joe's house.

Ginny pan-fried the pork chops and stir-fried the vegetables in the wok. Joe set the table and poured the wine. It was bedtime before either of them realized it.

Chapter 10

The weekend went by like it was on steroids. Both Ginny and Joe hoped to do some special things. This was their last weekend before they'd no longer be working together for several months. And Joe would start being away most of every week. The time went by quickly: Joe researching the DEA and other drug-enforcement activities on the internet, reading some of the background material the DEA had sent him, and packing for his week of orientation. Ginny stayed busy cleaning Joe's house, and then loading all the cleaning supplies in her car so she could thoroughly clean her condo Monday evening. They did manage to devote some time to discussions, dinner in a nice Italian restaurant Saturday night, and lovemaking both Saturday and Sunday nights.

Chapter 11

Joe was up bright and early Monday morning. With a one-hour drive to Cincinnati, he was out the door at 6:15. He drove about a half-hour before stopping for breakfast at a McDonalds right off US 75. Joe pulled into the office building's parking lot at about 7:40 and was in the designated conference room about five minutes later.

The conference room had been set up with three rows of two tables each, with three chairs at each table. There was a podium in front of the room and two tables, one holding coffee, water and donuts, in the rear of the room, adjacent to the door.

After helping himself to a cup of coffee and a donut, Joe introduced himself to a few of the attendees and to the instructor, then grabbed the chair at the left corner of the left table in the last row.

At exactly eight o'clock, the instructor stood up behind the podium. "Good morning, everyone. I'm William Bailey, with the DEA Training Unit. I'm responsible for this orientation program. I'll be leading several of the sessions myself, but we'll be having other specialists in for several of the sessions. If you have any problems or issues, I'm the one to see. Let's first go through a few administrative and logistical details."

Bailey spent the next ten minutes describing a wide variety of practical details: the location of exits, fire exits and restrooms; the daily schedule; the requirement that all cellphones be off or on mute; the fact that breakfast would be provided for all at the hotel, as would lunch in the cafeteria in the basement of the building they were in — they were on their own for dinners. He also informed the attendees that they had been pre-registered at the Hampton Inn a few miles away, with their rooms and roommates already assigned. All the attendees needed to do was pick up their key at the front desk. He recommended they drive to the hotel at the end of the first day and leave their cars parked there until Friday; it would be easier and quicker for them to share taxis for the four-mile ride between the DEA offices and the hotel.

"Any questions?"

"I have one. What if we need a pee break in the middle of a class?"

"Just get up and go to the john. We're all grown up enough that you don't need to raise your hand first, and we don't issue hall passes."

Everyone laughed at that, except for the red-faced officer who had asked the question.

"Any other questions? None. Good. OK, let's go around the room now. Each of you should state your name, your location, the organization you're affiliated with, the task force you'll be joining and whatever other pearls you'd like to share with the rest of us."

It took about 45 minutes to get through the 13 attendees. Joe followed along by reading the short bio of each attendee provided in the material that had been sent to him. As each person spoke, Joe made an occasional note next to the printed information. He paid special attention to Billy Vegas, his roommate. Of the 13 attendees, three of whom were female, slightly more than half were from various sheriff's offices, city police departments or the Highway Patrol and were being assigned full-time to a task force. The remainder were state or federal law enforcement folks who'd be working part-time with one or a few task forces, either as a member or a support specialist.

"OK, let's spend a few minutes going over the planned sessions for the week. After that, we'll take a short break and then get into it."

Joe was impressed with how organized the preparations were and how thorough the course outline was. They seemed to cover everything he could think to ask about task forces, the DEA and the so-called war on drugs. There seemed to be a lot of material on understanding each of the many different drugs — the illegal as well as the legally prescribed. Joe hoped he could keep up with those presentations. *Man, I never was good with that chemistry and biology stuff in school. And I sure am out of practice sitting in a classroom for a solid week. Wonder if this week'll be tougher on my brain or my ass.*

The rest of the day went by much faster than Joe had expected. Up until lunchtime, the lectures dealt with task forces in general and drug task forces in particular. Bailey talked about the history of and reasons for task forces, the differences between permanent and temporary ones, and the various intricacies of working through and around the bureaucracy and communications problems often associated with task forces.

Bailey then spent time describing the Drug Enforcement Agency and its leadership of drug task forces all over the country.

"The DEA, formed in 1973, is the only single-mission federal agency dedicated to drug law enforcement. The DEA's 9,000 employees work out of more than 200 domestic and almost 90 overseas offices. We're currently managing more than 250 state and local task forces across the US. Of these, about 30 are High Intensity Drug Trafficking Areas. These HIDTAs, as they're called, exist in the most significant centers of illegal drug activities."

"I'm assigned to one of these HIDTAs," said the attendee sitting next to Joe.

"Don't get too excited about that," said Bailey. "So are about half the folks in the room. One more thing — all state and local officers on our task forces get deputized to perform all the functions of our agents. OK, let's break for lunch now. I'll lead the way to the cafeteria. You can take whatever, and as much as you want. The cashier has your names and knows to charge your meals to this orientation course. Back here in an hour."

Joe was pleasantly surprised with the variety and quality of the food. He had a freshly made turkey club sandwich with a side salad and a Diet Coke. He enjoyed sitting with a few classmates, everyone getting to know each other and sharing war stories.

After lunch, Bailey introduced one of the DEA Investigators, who spent the entire afternoon explaining narcotics, hallucinogens, stimulants and depressants. He talked about their chemistries, their effects on humans, the brand and street names of the most common drugs in each category and which were the most widespread in terms of abuse. Joe had trouble understanding some and remembering much of the presentation, and his notetaking couldn't keep up. Fortunately, most of the information was included in the handouts.

Finally, class ended. Everyone except two who lived fairly local drove to the hotel and checked in. Joe and Vegas selected their beds and unpacked. They met the others in the lobby, and they all walked two blocks to an Outback Steakhouse for dinner. Joe enjoyed his steak and baked potato, but they were minor enjoyments compared to his two beers. Joe was pleased to hear that everyone else had as much trouble with the afternoon lecture as he had.

Back in his room, Joe called Ginny. It was good to hear her voice. He gave her a rundown of his day, being reserved with what he said as Vegas was sitting five feet away on his bed.

"Good to hear your voice, Joe. It was weird today. I'm so used to us being together, and working together, all day. I mean, Caruso's fine. But it's not the same as with you."

"I would hope not," said Joe with a chuckle.

"Not much progress with our missing schoolgirl. Caruso and I spent almost half the day talking with students and some more of Amy's current and former teachers. But we didn't really learn much."

"Hang in there. Something'll develop sooner or later."

"I know. And we're hanging. The good news is that I'm making a lot of progress cleaning and straightening up the condo. Hell, it's going to look so good, you and I might want to live here."

"Glad you're cleaning it up, but I don't think it's gonna be our future home."

"I know. Just saying. And, I'm going to sleep here tonight. Hadn't realized, but it'll be the first time in months. If I needed any other arguments to convince me to sell it, that realization will do it."

"Well, good for you. That's about it for now. I've got some heavy reading to do, all about the chemistry and biology of different drugs. Then it's off to bed."

"OK. Happy studying. And good night. Hope your roommate doesn't snore too loud."

"Can't be any worse than you."

"Joe. You know I don't —"

"I know. I know. Just teasing ya. Good night. Love you."

"Love you back. And miss you."

Joe and Vegas spent a little over an hour studying, then got ready for bed. Both fell asleep almost immediately.

Chapter 12

Ginny got to work around eight the next morning. Caruso was already hard at work at his desk.

"Morning, Ginny."

"Good morning. You look like you're deep into something."

"Yeah. I'm frustrated with us being stuck. I'm reading through the entire file again, hoping something new will jump out at me."

"Worth a try. Give a yell if you have any questions or see something we missed."

"Will do."

Around 10:15, Ginny's phone rang, and she reached to pick it up. *Bet it's Joe calling to say good morning.*

"Good morning, Joe."

"Detective? Detective Harris? This isn't Joe. This is Mrs. Franley. From Pond View Girls Academy."

"Oh. So sorry. I was expecting another call. What can we help you with, Mrs. Franley?"

"I think we have another one."

"Another what?"

"Missing person. This time it's Howard Newman, one of our chemistry teachers. I believe you interviewed him a few days ago."

"Oh? Yes, we did interview him on Friday. What happened?"

"No idea. That's why I'm calling you. He never showed up for his classes yesterday. No answer on his cellphone — we tried and left voicemail messages several times. One of our assistants even drove to his house this morning. It was locked and no one answered the door. She couldn't see whether or not his car was in the garage. What's going on?"

"Stay calm, Mrs. Franley. You did the right thing calling. We're leaving right now and will see you shortly."

"OK. Thank you."

Ginny hung up the phone and said to Caruso, "Let's go."

"Where?"

"Pond View Academy. That was Mrs. Franley, the head of the place. Thinks someone else is now missing. One of the teachers this time. Mr. Newman, in fact."

Putting their coats on, Caruso followed Ginny to her car. Thirty minutes later, they were walking into the administration building.

Approaching the receptionist, Ginny said, "Hi, again. I'm Detective Harris and this is Detective Caruso. We're here to see Mrs. Franley. She's expecting us."

"Yes, I know. Mrs. Franley told me to bring you to her office as soon as you arrived."

As they walked into Franley's office, Franley stood up, walked around her desk and led Ginny and Caruso to the same area where Ginny and Joe had sat a week ago.

"OK, Mrs. Franley. Please tell us exactly what happened, and when and how you found out."

"Yes. Of course. It started with a text from Rita LaForte. You'll recall she's our academic dean. Some places would call her provost, but that seems a bit stuffy to us. She sent me the text late yesterday morning. It said that Howard Newman, one of our three chemistry teachers, was out, but that she had juggled schedules to be sure his classes were covered. I thought little of it, other than I was glad she managed to cover his schedule and was keeping me informed of what was going on. Some of the staff seem to forget this, no matter how often I remind them. I wondered why he was absent, but I soon got busy with other things. Anyhow, Mr. Newman's absence seemed under control, and I thought no more of it."

"And then?" asked Ginny.

"Rita came to see me this morning. Just a few minutes before I called you."

"Yes? And?"

"She told me that they never heard from Mr. Newman at all yesterday. He never returned any of the phone or text messages they left. Then, he didn't show up for classes this morning either. When he again didn't answer his phone, she sent her administrative assistant to his house, but she learned nothing."

"Did it look like he was home?" asked Caruso.

"She couldn't be sure. No one answered the doorbell. And his garage has no windows, so she couldn't tell if his car was there."

"I see."

"And that's when I decided to call you."

"Mrs. Franley, were Mr. Newman and Amy unusually close?" asked Caruso.

"What! Are you suggesting what I think you are? No way. Mr. Newman has taught here for five years. And we've never had any type of trouble with him. Especially along the lines of what you're implying."

"Mrs. Franley, I'm not implying anything. But we can't just ignore certain possibilities either, no matter how distasteful they may be."

"Yes, yes. I understand. You just threw me for a second. But I'd be shocked if there was anything inappropriate going on between Amy and Mr. Newman."

"How can you be so sure?" asked Ginny.

"This is a small, close-knit community. It's difficult to do almost anything without some of the students or staff becoming aware of it. Or at least suspecting something."

"Fair enough. We'd like to speak with Mrs. LaForte, as well as her assistant who went out to Mr. Newman's house. We'd also like to speak with some of his colleagues. Especially those he was most friendly with. And finally, please give us his home address. We'd like to check out his house for ourselves. And speak with his wife."

"I can't help you with that last item."

"Oh?" said Caruso.

"Mr. Newman got divorced about a year ago. His wife got involved with some other man. I think she wound up marrying him and moving out of state. I don't know where. Heck, I don't even know her new last name."

"That's OK. We have ways of tracking her down," said Caruso.

"We're going to take a quick run out to the professor's house," said Ginny. "We can force entry to do a wellness check without a search warrant. So we'll at least know if he's home, perhaps severely ill or injured, or worse. We'll then return here and conduct the interviews. Perhaps we could start with Mrs. LaForte, and then her assistant."

"That would be fine. I sure hope he's OK."

Ginny and Caruso headed to Newman's house. Along the way, Caruso called and spoke with one of the assistant prosecuting attorneys. Caruso explained Newman's disappearance, gave her Newman's address, explained that they were on their way there to conduct a wellness check, but they wanted an expedited search warrant so that they and the crime scene techs could return later in the day and thoroughly search Newman's house and belongings, including his phones and laptop computer — assuming they were there. At the same time, Ginny called the desk sergeant and asked him to again have the pond near the school and surrounding woods searched, this time for Newman rather than Amy.

It was only about a ten-minute drive. Ginny parked in front of a small, split-level house, wrapped in panels of light-yellow vinyl siding. The front lawn was small. The front door had sidelights on both sides. Ginny looked in but saw only an unoccupied living room. Ringing the bell accomplished nothing.

Ginny and Caruso checked with a few neighbors. None of them knew anything about Newman being missing. They all assumed he was at work, teaching, as he did every school day. None of them had ever seen Newman with a woman or girl, other than his wife prior to their divorce. The divorce was apparently civil, but no one knew any of the details.

Caruso forced open the rear door to Newman's house. A quick inspection revealed that Newman was not there, but his car was in the garage. Careful not to inspect anything that wasn't in plain sight, the detectives left, planning to return later in the day with the CSI techs once the search warrant was issued.

The detectives returned to the school. They went to Franley's office to tell her Newman was not in his house and that they were ready to conduct the interviews.

"Fine." Franley told her assistant the various people whom the detectives would like to talk with. She asked her assistant to find an empty office for the detectives to use, and to start organizing the interviews.

"On a somewhat separate note, thanks for the advance notice about the press conference last week. Have any worthwhile leads developed from that?"

"Not yet. But we're still following up several of the phone calls we received."

Ginny and Caruso settled into the empty office they were provided and spent the next three hours conducting a steady stream of interviews. Fortunately, Franley's assistant brought them nice, large salads for lunch. No one had seen nor heard about anything inappropriate in Newman's relationship with Amy, and none of them could believe that Newman would act that way, not even if Amy had tempted and encouraged him. In fact, one of the other chemistry teachers said she suspected that Newman was actually gay, and that might have been the underlying cause of his divorce.

Two of Newman's colleagues, Mr. Gardner, one of the history teachers, and Ms. DuBois, one of the French teachers, mentioned that Newman often spoke very highly of Amy and met with her after class hours in his office a number of times. But they were both adamant that they were sure no inappropriate behavior took place.

"OK, Denny, I think we've learned all we can for now here."

Ginny and Caruso said good-bye to Franley and her assistant and returned to headquarters and their desks. Ginny called the crime scene group and asked that they join Caruso and her at Newman's house as soon as the search warrant came through.

It only took a few minutes for Ginny to check the county marriage records and find the name of the new husband of Newman's ex-wife. With his Jasper Creek former address in hand, Ginny and Caruso were soon questioning his former neighbors. They learned that after his fairly recent marriage, he and his new wife had moved to Tampa, Florida. His Jasper Creek home was still for sale. Ginny found the Tampa address and phone number, and was soon speaking with the ex-Mrs. Newman on the phone.

"Hello."

"Hello, is this Mrs. Yolanski? This is Detective Harris, with the Jasper Creek Police Department."

"Yes? How can I help you?"

"I'm calling about your ex-husband."

"Oh? Is something wrong? Did something happen to Howard?"

"We're not sure. He hasn't shown up at school these past two days, and no one's been able to get in touch with him."

"That's very unusual. It's not like Howard. He's always

been exceptionally disciplined about his work. And dedicated."

"Any idea where he might have gone? Or with whom?"

"No. Sorry. But I can't imagine."

"Mrs. Yolanski, I need to ask you a few personal questions. I hope you won't mind."

"Go ahead."

"What was the reason for your divorce?"

"Wow. You really do mean personal. It's hard to describe. It wasn't anything specific. We just gradually grew apart."

"Mrs. Yolanski, we were told that you left him for another man. Who you've since married."

"What a bunch of blabbermouths. For the record, my new, uh, relationship began only after Howard and I agreed to divorce. Your so-called sources probably didn't know that little detail."

"Mrs. Yolanski, was there ever an issue with Mr. Newman having what you'd call a relationship with someone else?"

"What! No. At least not that I was ever aware of."

"Ever any evidence or rumors of his being involved with any of his students?"

"Definitely not. Howard wasn't like that."

"One more question. Was your husband gay?"

"What! Where'd you get that? No way. I mean, even though we never had kids, we had a regular sex life. I don't think that would have been true if he were gay. Do you?"

"No, I'd think not. Well, thank you for your help. Let me give you my phone number. Please call me if you hear from your ex-husband or if you think of anything else."

"OK."

Ginny gave Yolanski her phone number and ended the call. She filled in Caruso, and both agreed they still didn't have much to work with.

Later that afternoon, Ginny and Caruso were back inside Newman's house, along with three crime scene technicians and a search warrant. While the technicians checked for blood, fingerprints, forced entry and other physical clues, Ginny and Caruso went through the papers they found on Newman's desk and in a short filing cabinet next to the desk. They found nothing unusual. The crime scene techs went thoroughly over Newman's car in the garage but came up with nothing suspicious. They took a number of fingerprints off the car, but, as they all looked just like the fingerprints found throughout the house, it was assumed they belonged to Newman. Before they left, Ginny asked the technicians to be sure to take Newman's laptop downtown for the IT group to search for some hoped-for clues.

Having already canvassed the neighbors, and seeing no cameras in the residential neighborhood, Ginny and Caruso returned to the station. Ginny again called the taxi companies, this time inquiring about a pickup in Newman's neighborhood, but none of the companies had made such a pickup in the past week. At about 4:30, the desk sergeant called Ginny to say that their search of the pond and its surroundings again came up empty.

Five o'clock rolled around and Ginny and Caruso left work. Ginny headed to her condo for a quick dinner and then her meeting with the first of the three realtors she had scheduled for that week.

Chapter 13

The first realtor arrived promptly at 6:30. She had a good opportunity to look around the condo and ask Ginny questions about the location. Her credentials — so she unsurprisingly claimed — were impeccable. She reaffirmed her appointment to return on Saturday with a customized presentation, and left about an hour after she'd arrived.

Ginny had just sat down to watch TV when the phone rang.

"Hello, is this that super-sleuth detective, Virginia Harris?"

"Joe! So good to hear from you. Feels like I haven't seen you in weeks."

"I know. I feel the same way. But, actually, I only left yesterday morning."

"Yeah, well, it feels a lot longer."

"I agree. I'm calling now 'cause my roommate's downstairs having a couple of beers with some of the others. Fill me in on everything, then I'll do the same for you."

"Deal. OK, I'll start with the easy one first." Ginny briefly described her earlier session with the realtor, then reminded Joe that she'd be seeing two more, and then all three would be back to meet with her and Joe on Saturday.

"So far so good. Glad we're finally past just talking about this and are finally actually doing it. I can't wait to see the prices they come up with."

"Me neither. And I hope picking the right realtor will be easy."

"OK. Now, about work. How's it going with Caruso?"

"Fine. As we've said, he's one of the good guys. Turns out he also seems to be a pretty decent detective, despite us not having much to show yet, which I'll get into in a minute. But, most importantly, as great as he is, I'm still planning on marrying you."

"Glad to hear that. My roommate's also pretty good, but I think I prefer you."

"Nice to know that I beat out your male roommate," said Ginny with a laugh.

"So, where are you with the case? Did Amy just run off, or is it something more than that?"

"Sadly, no big breakthrough on that. At least not yet. But, as we've said, going this long without hearing from any abductor makes it increasingly likely that either she ran away or was abducted for a reason other than kidnapping-for-ransom. God, I hate to even consider those gruesome murder or sex slave or teenager-for-sale alternatives."

"I agree with you on that. But these days, anything is possible."

"Yeah, I know. But there's more."

"Oh?"

"Turns out that one of the male teachers at Pond View is now also missing. Didn't show up for his classes yesterday or today, and can't be reached or located."

"Maybe it's all an elaborate plot — he and Amy run off separately, but hook up together later."

"Yeah, that's on our list of possibilities. But everyone

we've spoken with says that'd be totally out of character for him. On the other hand, he is recently divorced, so…"

"Is he one of Amy's teachers?"

"Was last year, but not this year. Yet Amy continued going to his office after classes were over even though she's not in his class this year. Despite what everyone says, Denny and I aren't at all sure there wasn't something more than studying chemical formulas going on."

"Umm. Sounds like you have your hands full. Wish I was there to work the case with you."

"Yeah, me too. But it is what it is. Now tell me about your day."

"This morning's sessions were pretty easy going. They talked about the various groups within a task force. But they intentionally kept it pretty general because each task force is organized slightly different than the others."

"Makes sense. I guess each one organizes to maximize its own efficiency."

"Yeah, that sounds good in theory. I'm curious to see if it actually works as well in practice."

"Oh, ye of little faith."

"Or maybe I've just learned things from my past experiences. Anyhow, the rest of the morning then dealt with administration. All the necessary, but often unseen, functions like human resources, purchasing, providing funds for drug buys and on and on and on."

"Like you say, unglamorous, but needed."

"Yup. Anyhow, things got more interesting in the afternoon. They had a couple of different speakers, one from the DEA in Washington and one working on a drug task force in Pennsylvania. They talked about Drug Diversion.

That deals with the huge problem of prescription drugs. Everything from doctors who write way too many prescriptions, to so-called doctor shopping to get multiple prescriptions, to certain pharmacies dispensing many times the normal amount of these drugs."

"Yeah. When most people hear drug abuse, they think of the drug cartels in Mexico and Central America. But prescribed drugs are also a huge problem."

"For sure. I mean, I knew about it in general, but the numbers and statistics they presented were mind-boggling."

"Sounds like a good session."

"It was. They also covered some of the cases they've broken, and some of the ways they analyze data to identify the problem doctors and pharmacies. They often use undercover work to gather the evidence needed for a conviction."

"Wow, they covered a lot of ground in one day."

"They did. And I sort of surprised myself. Knowing I'll be here just temporarily, and my real objective, I expected I'd just half-listen this week to get a general idea of things. But I'm into it. I don't think of myself as competitive, but I find myself trying to keep up with it all. I'd like to wind up near the head of the class."

"Joe, are you kidding? You're one of the most competitive people I know. The difference is you compete fairly, and you're really competing internally against yourself, not against others. You want to prove to yourself that you can do it, or that you're number one, or whatever."

"Yeah, maybe. But I never thought or realized that before."

"Just think of me as your own private mirror. You can ask questions. 'Mirror, mirror on the wall, who's the greatest… whatever?'"

"OK, mirror. Enough psychobabble for one night. Time to hit the sack so I'm rested enough to beat the rest of the pack tomorrow."

"Got it. Have a good night, Joe."

"Night. Love you."

"Love you too."

Chapter 14

The next three days went by very quickly for Joe. He found the lectures interesting and informative.

Wednesday's lectures dealt with most of the major operational parts of task forces: the Highway Interdiction unit responsible for intercepting the transport of illicit drugs into and through the task force's geographical territory; the Undercover Group which arranges drug buys and conducts surveillance; the Drug Diversion team which deals with prescription drugs; and the Investigation Group which is responsible for the analyses of financial, telephone and other records, as well as identifying the key personnel of drug trafficking organizations.

Thursday was largely devoted to various drug-related crimes, the differences between federal and state charges and which apply when, and the prison terms applicable to various federal and state drug charges. Just before class ended on Thursday, everyone was reminded to check out of the hotel Friday morning as the course would end sometime mid-afternoon on Friday.

On Friday morning, the class heard from four drug task force members describing their functions on their task force, how they performed their jobs and how they interacted with other parts of the task force and non-task force law enforcement agencies. These functions included testing by forensic and chemical labs and surveillance by the Highway Patrol Aviation Unit. This was probably among the most interesting sessions to Joe.

Lunch was a surprise mini-banquet, served in a private room at one end of the cafeteria. It ended with short speeches by Bailey and a few other DEA employees, and distribution of course-completion certificates to all the attendees. Some good-natured ribbing, wishes of good luck and promises to stay in touch, and the session ended. Joe was on the road heading back to Jasper Creek by 2:30.

///////////

Unfortunately, the week dragged on much more slowly for Ginny and Caruso. The highlights of Ginny's week were meetings with the two additional realtors at her condo. Not much progress was made on the two missing persons from the girls' academy.

Ginny checked with IT to see if they found anything interesting on Newman's laptop.

"What a boring life. Poor guy."

"Why do you say that?" asked Ginny.

"If you assume what's on his laptop bears some reflection of what his life was like, boring, boring, boring."

"Oh?"

"Yeah, virtually no e-mails other than those related to work — schedule changes, assignments for his students, answering a few students' questions, and faculty stuff. No social media use at all, not even any accounts set up. The only bookmarked websites dealt with chemistry, chemistry conferences and teaching-related stuff. His only online purchases seemed to be an occasional chemistry book from Amazon."

"I see what you mean. Not the wildest life ever."

"Indeed. Sorry, Ginny, but we couldn't find anything to help you."

"Not your fault. You can only find what's there. Anyhow, appreciate the effort."

"Don't mention it."

The unexpected second press conference was a surprise to both Ginny and Caruso.

"I don't care," said the chief. "I'm telling you we have to have a press conference about the missing teacher."

"But, Chief," said Caruso. "We don't know a damn thing yet. Why have a press conference to say that we have nothing to say?"

"That's one way to look at it. But not the right way."

"How do you see it, Chief?" asked Ginny.

"Look. His being missing is not going to remain a secret much longer. Too many people know about it. It's gonna hit the media anytime now."

"Agreed," said Ginny.

"And when it does, all kinds of rumors and theories, including crazy conspiracies, are going to spring up. If we have to say 'we have nothing to report,' or more likely something along the lines of 'we are actively pursuing several lines of inquiry and do not want to divulge any details at this time,' we're a lot better off proactively saying it than mumbling it in response to a question thrown at us."

"I see your point," said Caruso.

"Chief, whenever you're ready to enter politics, you got my vote," said Ginny.

"Enter politics? What are you talking about? I've been up to my butt in politics ever since I took this chief's job."

"Who'll lead the press conference?" asked Ginny.

"I'd say the lead detective. That's you, Ginny. I'll be there to show my support, as will Caruso here, but you'll be the star performer."

"My lucky day," said Ginny.

And perform she did. The press conference was set for ten o'clock on Thursday morning, in the PD headquarters lobby. The whole thing lasted less than twenty minutes. Ginny had little to announce, and even less to say in response to questions. The media folks left a bit disappointed, but they were used to the authorities refusing to discuss an ongoing investigation. The TV news that evening and the newspapers the next morning gave Newman's disappearance a lot of coverage but provided few facts. A few outlets referenced Amy's disappearance and asked whether the two cases might be related, but that was the extent of it.

The police received several calls that evening and the next day about Newman's disappearance, but far fewer than Amy's press conference had generated. None of the calls led to anything useful.

The week ended with both Caruso and Ginny disappointed. They were out of ideas as to where to look next and were getting more and more frustrated by their lack of leads. Increasingly, they worried about not making any progress before someone else from the school went missing. *Are we dealing with a serial abductor?* thought Ginny.

Ninety minutes later, Ginny was just sitting down to a cheese-omelette-and-salad extra-late lunch at the counter in Joe's kitchen, when Joe walked in.

Ginny jumped up and ran into Joe's arms. "What a great surprise! I didn't expect you for a few hours yet. So glad you're home for the weekend."

While kissing, Joe mumbled something that sounded like, "Me too." He then explained the surprise luncheon and how things wrapped up mid-afternoon.

Ginny covered her omelette to keep it warm and prepared and fried a twin for Joe.

They both ate lunch, a late one for Ginny and a second one for Joe, washing it down with beer. They then filled each other in on the just-completed work week, agreeing to leave more complete discussions for Saturday and Sunday. Ginny told Joe that the three realtors would be meeting them at her condo the next day, one each at 12, two and four o'clock. One TV show and they were soon in bed, feeling as if they had weeks of separation to make up for.

Chapter 15

Saturday morning, Joe and Ginny slept until nine o'clock, a rare luxury for them. They had breakfast at a local diner, then went to the supermarket to restock Joe's refrigerator, as well as to pick up two pre-made salads and a six-pack of beer for their afternoon vigil at Ginny's condo.

About five minutes before twelve, Ginny answered the doorbell and welcomed the first of the realtors.

"Hi, Susan. Nice to see you again."

"Hi, Ginny."

Ginny introduced the realtor and Joe to each other. They then spent about a half-hour with Susan leading Ginny and Joe through the material she had assembled into folders for each of them. Based on nearby comps, Susan stated her belief that they should be able to sell Ginny's condo for about $194,500 and it might take up to 90 days from start to closing. Susan suggested that they list the condo at $209,900 so that they'd have some negotiating room. She then spent the last five minutes describing her background and track record, the resources of the agency she worked for and why she and her agency were better than the competition.

Ginny committed to selecting a realtor within the next few days, at which time she'd be back in touch with Susan.

As soon as Susan left and Ginny closed the door, she turned to Joe with a big smile on her face. "Wow. $194,000 and change. That's a lot higher than the $150,000 we were thinking of."

"Sure is. But who knows if it's real? Hell, we don't even know if she really believes that price, or just threw it out there to entice us into hiring her."

"Boy, you sure can spoil things fast. Just kidding. I know you're right. Let's gobble down our lunch and get ready for number two. Oh, damn. I forgot to ask her what changes or fixing-up or whatever she'd recommend we do here before we put it on the market."

"Well, let's remember to ask the next two. I'm sure the answers'll be pretty much the same for all of them."

The two o'clock realtor was also there about an hour. The session was quite similar to the one with Susan, with one exception. Claiming the large number of similar nearby condos for sale was becoming a drag on the market, he said it was important to try to sell the unit quickly before the market viewed the listing as "old." And to do that, he recommended listing it at $134,900. This obviously was disappointing to Ginny and Joe. On the other hand, they were relieved to hear the realtor's opinion that other than a thorough cleaning, the removal of some of Ginny's clothing, papers and nick-nacks (as well as the recliner to make the living room look larger), little needed to be done with the condo to make it more salable.

While Ginny was showing the second realtor out, Joe excused himself to answer a phone call.

"Detective McFarland."

"Hello, Detective. This is Pete Singleton, with the Drug Enforcement Administration here in Youngstown."

"Hello, sir."

"Sorry to bother you on the weekend, but it's been that kind of a week."

"Not a problem."

"First off, I want to congratulate you on making it through the orientation program. I know they cram a lot of info into five days."

"Thank you. And yes, they do. In fact, I've got most of tomorrow reserved for going back over my notes and all the material they handed out."

"Not surprised. The other reason for my call, Joe, is that I wanted to arrange for us to have a chat Monday morning before you settle in as a task force member."

"I'd be happy to. Just say where and when."

"How about my office here in Youngstown? Say 0800. I'll tell the folks at the task force in Medina that you'll be arriving late. At my insistence. Let me give you my address."

"No need. My chief gave me your address and phone number before orientation began."

"Good for him. OK, then. See you Monday morning."

"I'll be there."

Joe returned to the living room and sat down next to Ginny to await the third realtor. She arrived right on time at four o'clock. It didn't take long for them to conclude that Mary Beth, the third realtor, was the winner. She had the most polished presentation, predicted a price-range of $145,000 to $160,000 and a time-to-closing of 75 to 120 days. She also described in detail the marketing program she would put together, starting with a brokers' open house, with catered sandwiches and salads to ensure a large turnout. She also indicated that, although major changes to the condo weren't required, one of her colleagues at her agency focused on the so-called staging of properties for sale, and she would come by and work with Ginny if Ginny selected Mary Beth.

After Mary Beth left, Joe said, "Seems like a no-brainer to me. Mary Beth gets my vote."

"Mine also. Besides her estimated price being in the middle and most likely the most accurate, I like that she presented a price range, as well as a time range. Seems more realistic than a specific number."

"Agreed."

"I say we sleep on it tonight and, if we still feel this way, I'll get the ball rolling tomorrow. Yikes, all of a sudden, it's getting real."

"Having second thoughts?"

"No. It's the right thing to do. I'm just being an emotional female for a few minutes. Is that allowed?"

"Sure is. And I understand it. Even though you haven't been here much recently, it has been your home for years."

"OK, I'm set. What say we stop for some sushi on our way back to your place?"

"Works for me."

Chapter 16

Joe spent Sunday morning reviewing his notes and the handouts from the orientation program. He felt pretty good about the material — except for most of the chemical and biological details of each of the many drugs the task force would be dealing with. Despite his undercover assignment, Joe knew he'd have to perform as a normal member of the task force, and he was too proud to not perform well.

Ginny spent half the morning making two trips to her condo and back, each time returning to Joe's house with her car loaded with clothing and other possessions. She wanted to get a jump on preparing the condo for going on the market. Before sitting down for lunch, Ginny and Joe both confirmed they still favored Mary Beth. Ginny called her, and she was delighted to have been selected. She promised to get all the necessary paperwork to Ginny no later than midweek, and to begin scheduling the open house and other marketing activities. Ginny then called the other two realtors with the news that someone else had been selected. They both were disappointed, but acted totally professionally.

Joe was surprised at how quickly Ginny's possessions were filling up his house, but he was glad the process of selling her condo was finally underway.

After lunch, Ginny and Joe spent almost two hours talking through the two missing persons from Pond

View Girls Academy. Ginny described everything she and Caruso had done following up on Amy's — and then Howard Newman's — disappearances. Joe asked several questions and posed a number of theories. But in the end, he had little new to offer Ginny in terms of next steps or other avenues to explore. His largest contribution was to reassure Ginny she wasn't missing anything, and to remind her that she and Joe had been in a similar position on several past cases. Almost every time, something developed which allowed them to solve the case.

"Denny and I do agree, Joe, that the two missing-person cases are somehow related. Too coincidental — both missing from the same school and the relationship, even if non-sexual, between the two."

"Yeah, and now all you have to do is figure out exactly how they are related."

Ginny made a large pot of spaghetti and meatballs, along with a salad, for dinner. Joe's contribution was opening a bottle of Chianti.

They went to bed early. Joe wanted to at least start his new assignment reasonably well-rested.

Chapter 17

*J*oe left home at four the next morning. Allowing for the possibility of traffic and time for a quick breakfast stop, he wanted to be sure not to be late for his eight o'clock meeting with RAC Singleton.

He was sitting in front of Singleton's desk at 7:40. Singleton was at his desk, and looked like he'd already been there a while. Joe was surprised by Singleton's appearance. Probably in his mid-fifties, short, somewhat overweight and bald. Singleton's frameless glasses only added to his looking more like an accountant or economics professor than a top law enforcement official.

"Morning, Joe. Appreciate your coming in. Coffee?"

"That'd be great. I've already had a few cups, but one more would be fine. Black, please."

Singleton buzzed his administrative assistant. A few minutes later, Singleton and Joe were each holding a large paper cup, filled with too-hot-to-drink coffee.

"Joe, beside us getting to know each other a bit personally, I wanted to discuss your undercover assignment."

"I'd appreciate that."

"Over the past several months, I've developed good reason to believe that more than one member of our task force has been dirty."

"Exactly how?"

"We're pretty sure we've had shortages in our inventory of seized drugs, as well as seized drug money. We've also had third-hand comments about task force members squeezing traffickers and over-prescribing docs for payoffs to avoid arrest."

"Damn. I hate to hear that. Do you know who the bad ones are?"

"I think I do. At least a couple of them. But it's more from listening to my gut than from hard evidence or solid identification."

"Well, our guts are often pretty darn reliable. Who do you suspect?"

"I'd rather not say. I don't want to bias your investigation. Or have you catch the few that I name and perhaps miss some others."

"I can understand that. How about telling me some of the specific incidents without naming names?"

"That's what I was planning to do. Let me first explain how your task force involvement will work. As I'm sure you heard during orientation, our task forces typically have a combination of full-time and part-time or support members, with personnel coming from the DEA, other federal agencies like the FBI, ATF and ICE, and several local and state law enforcement agencies. This task force has a total of about 25 members, and they're organized into four groups or departments: Drug Diversion, Field Operations, Intelligence, and Administration. As we do with most new task force members, your first several weeks will have you rotating through all of these groups to help you get an understanding of everything that we do and how the pieces fit together. You'll spend up to a week or so with each group. After that, you and I will decide where to next place you — in one of the departments, or maybe we just keep you rotating. We'll see, depending on what you learn in the meantime."

"That rotation sounds like a good way to start."

"One other thing. Only you, your chief and I know about your assignment. There are several managers on the task force who I trust. But I can't be totally one-hundred-percent positive, and I don't want to put you or your assignment at risk."

"Appreciate that. How and to whom do I report findings, ask questions, and so on?"

"That would be me. Suggest you call me on my cell. You have the number. If we can handle it by phone, great. If not, we can arrange to meet at some off-the-beaten-track place between here and Jasper Creek, or between here and Medina. Work for you?"

"Yes. That'll be fine."

"OK, then. Let's get you out of here. When you get to the Medina County Sheriff's Office, ask for Deputy Graham. He handles all the administrative stuff for the task force. He'll get you settled in." Singleton stood up, walked around his desk and stuck out his right hand. "Again, good to meet you, Joe. And good luck with this. Don't hesitate to call if you have any questions or problems."

"Will do. Thanks," said Joe as he stood up, shook hands with Singleton and then headed for the door.

Slightly more than an hour later, Joe pulled into the parking lot of the sheriff's office on Commerce Street in Medina. Five minutes later, he was in Graham's small office, enjoying yet another cup of coffee.

"Welcome to Medina, Joe. And to the task force."

"Thank you, sir."

"OK, you can drop the 'sir.' It's just plain Larry."

"Got it. Larry it is."

"Joe, since I handle most of the administrative stuff for the task force, my thinking is to have you spend your first week here going through, and helping out with, all the administrative stuff. If that's OK with you."

"Sure, that's fine. It's probably a good spot to get the best initial overview."

"Yeah, that's my thought. Let me first explain what I expect will be the most confusing item."

"Go for it. I'm ready."

"As you know, this is the sheriff's office here. And we do all the normal sheriff-like things for Medina County. We have jurisdiction across the whole county, but we usually don't get involved in the cities like Medina or Brunswick, which have their own PDs. Unless, of course, we're called in, or enter as part of one of our cases. Or as part of a chase."

"That's pretty standard."

"Yes, it is. But here's where it gets a bit involved. The county drug task force, as well as the DEA task force you're on, are both co-located here. And a number of the same people work for the sheriff's department and for one, and occasionally both, of the drug task forces."

"That's gotta get complicated."

"Yeah, it can. But it's our job in Administration to keep things straight and to untangle situations when they occur. And they do occur. We resolve conflicts where one person is wanted for more than one thing at the same time. We keep track of costs and which entity is paying for what. And we make sure that special units, like the

DEA's Aviation Unit, are made available to one of the task forces when they're needed."

"Sounds like you have enough to keep you busy."

"No question. But I'll be in good shape this week. I'll have you to assist us. Once we get you up to speed, that is."

"There must be a lot of BS and infighting among these groups."

"Actually, there's surprisingly little. I think it's because everyone here is interested in only one thing — catching the bad guys. And they each want to apply their skills to doing that. They couldn't care less about which group gets or takes credit, or who pays for what. They leave all that backroom stuff to us in Administration."

"Sounds good. Let's get started."

Graham introduced Joe to the full-time members of his group — an accounts payable clerk, a human resources supervisor and an HR clerk, as well as to Gretchen Werner, Graham's administrative assistant. It was she who kept the group — as well as Graham himself — organized, and managed everyone's assignments and schedules, as well as coordinated events such as drug busts, highway intercepts and so on.

By that first afternoon, Joe was already working with the administrative staff, learning by doing. He was surprised at how much was actually being done that was useful. *Glad to see we're doing more than just bureaucratic paper shuffling.*

The day was over before he realized it, and by six o'clock Joe was in unit 116 of the Sunset Lodge, where a room had been reserved for him. *Didn't realize I'd be spending all my evenings in a tiny motel room like this. First chance I get, I gotta find a small apartment.* After unpacking, Joe drove to a nearby Pizza Hut for dinner. He was soon back in his room, where he quickly fell asleep while watching TV.

Chapter 18

While Joe was meeting with Singleton and starting his task force assignment, Ginny's day got off to anything but a boring start. On her way to the office, she got a call from Caruso at about 7:30.

"Hi, Denny. You're up bright and early."

"Yeah. Well, that's often the best time for bad news."

"Uh oh. Whaddaya got?"

"They just found Newman's body."

"Oh. Shit! Where? Who found it?"

"Under some bushes at the edge of Crystal Lake. Couple of early morning fisherman. One went to take a leak in the bushes. And surprise, surprise."

"You there now?"

"On my way. Call came in about ten minutes ago. I heard as soon as I walked in."

"Any news about Amy? Or, God forbid, her body?"

"Nope. At least not yet."

"OK. I'm turning around now. See you there."

"Fine. Park by the boat ramp. It's about a hundred yards east of the scene. I'm sure we'll see all the action when we pull in."

"Yup. See you in a few." *Damn, Joe was right when he predicted something would break in the case. Just didn't expect — or want — this kind of break.*

Twenty minutes later, Ginny parked opposite the boat

ramp at Crystal Lake. She was glad she kept a heavy jacket and gloves in the trunk of her car. The sky was dark and threatening, and a strong March wind was blowing inland from the lake — wet and cold. The ground was covered by a thin and patchy layer of snow.

She spotted "the troops" gathered in the area Caruso had indicated. She walked over and said good morning to Caruso, then gave a loud hello to everyone.

"Hi, Ginny," said the medical examiner. "Where's your sidekick? I thought you and Joe were chained together at the hip. What, you dump him for Caruso?"

"Yup. But just temporarily — and just professionally. Joe's been assigned to a drug task force."

"Good for him. Glad to see he's moving up in the world. Give him my congrats."

"Will do. Meanwhile, whadda we have here?"

"Blunt force to the back of his head. Looks like this is the dump site, not the crime scene."

"About how long?"

"Hard to say, what with the cold weather. But I'd guess four or five days. Or thereabouts."

"ID?"

"Yeah," answered Caruso. "Wallet in his pocket. Driver's license confirms it's Howard Newman. By the way, still had cash in the wallet. Clearly not a robbery gone bad."

"Not surprised. Where're the guys that found him?"

"Back near where you parked. Two guys sitting in the dirty white Ford pickup. Other than a few basics, I held off questioning them until you got here."

"Thanks, Denny. Let's go talk to them now."

Ginny and Caruso walked back to the parking area.

Caruso knocked on the driver's window and the man sitting behind the steering wheel rolled down the window.

"Mr. Stevens. Mr. Elwood. This is my partner, Detective Harris. We have a few more questions for you."

"Sure," said Stevens. Both men got out of the pickup and they and the two detectives stood in front of the truck.

"Which one of you first found the body?" asked Ginny.

"Me," said Elwood.

"Want to tell us in detail what happened? From the beginning."

"Sure. But not much to tell. We got here about seven this morning to get in some early morning fishing."

"You often do that?" asked Ginny.

"Depends on what you mean by often. We usually do it once or twice a week, unless the weather's really bad. We both work over at Gates Plastics. Second shift, from three in the afternoon 'til eleven. So our mornings are free, and we like to come here during the week 'cuz it's usually pretty deserted. Not like the crowds they get on weekends. Specially in the warm weather. But we like fishing here this time of year. The lake's still frozen, but the ice is thin enough at the edge that we can easily break through it. Sort a like ice fishing but without spending hours on a frozen lake."

"And what happened after you arrived this morning?" prompted Ginny.

"Like I said, we got here about seven. Took all our stuff from the truck down to the lake, just about 30 feet from where that body is."

"Then what happened?" asked Caruso.

"Before we actually started fishing, I decided to empty

my bladder of all the coffee I'd been drinking. Hate to just start fishing and then haveta stop and take a leak, if you know what I mean."

"Yes, we do, Mr. Elwood."

"I put my gear on the bank and walked over to those bushes. Trying to be a little discrete like. Anyhow, I damn near peed on myself. I was just getting down to business, so to say. I looked down and there he, or it, was. Just looking up at me. I'll never forget that. Scared the bejeezus out of me. I musta screamed, 'cause he was right next to me in seconds."

"Mr. Stevens?"

"Yeah. I heard him scream. Had no idea what the problem was. Thought maybe he was bit by a snake. I ran over to see if I could help. That's when I saw the body."

"That's exactly what happened. Then I called 9-1-1 on my cellphone, and we went to go sit in our truck 'til the police got here."

"Did you recognize the dead person? Ever see him before? Was there anyone else here around then?"

"No to all those questions," said Stevens.

"OK, thanks for your help. Here are our cards, if you think of anything else. We'll have one of our officers get your contact info in case we have more questions. Then you'll be free to go. Unless you want to continue your fishing this morning."

"No thanks. We've had enough for one day. We'll just head on home when the officer's finished with us."

"Fine. And thanks again," said Caruso.

Ginny and Caruso spoke with the first-on-scene officer,

but he had nothing to add to what the two fishermen had said. They also checked with the crime scene techs, but it was too soon to know much. They were spending most of their time making molds of various tire tracks in the parking area next to the boat ramp. Ginny made sure they knew about Amy, who may have been abducted by the same person or persons who took Newman, and emphasized the need for them to conduct a wide and thorough search by the lake in case she was also murdered and dumped in the area. She also asked that they get the cellphone found in Newman's coat pocket to the IT guys as soon as they got back to town.

"OK, Denny. Not much more for us to do here. See you back at the ranch. Guess our first step will be to bring the chief up to speed."

"Yup. See you there."

A short while later, the two detectives were giving the chief a detailed summary of that morning's developments at the lake.

"Too bad. But at least something happened. I was beginning to think this case was just frozen in time."

"But, Chief —"

"I know, Ginny. You were about to tell me all the things you're doing and analyzing. No need. That's what you get paid for, and that's what I assume you were and are doing. Any news about the missing girl from that school?"

"Amy Richardson. No, nothing. I made sure the CSI folks knew to do a thorough search of the lake area, just in case…"

"Good. But let's hope they don't find her."

"Agreed. Chief, we're getting increasingly worried about her. It's been two weeks and we haven't heard anything. Nada. Clearly not your typical kidnapping."

"Clearly not, indeed. But we gotta get a break before we find her body, or before she's forced into prostitution here or overseas, or sold to some wealthy pervert in the Far East. Not to mention before a third person, most likely from that same school, goes missing."

"You don't have to tell us, Chief. We've been worrying about exactly those things. Time sure as hell is not our friend."

"Yeah. And there'll be a feeding frenzy once the press gets hold of the news of Newman's body. And that'll be happening very soon. We need a quickie press conference to announce finding his body. That's the only way we can stay ahead of the press. Stay nearby. You two will be our guest speakers. No family or next of kin we need to inform first, correct?"

"Correct. But we probably should give his ex-wife, who lives out of state, and his employer at the school a heads-up, just as a courtesy."

"OK, why don't you two do that? I'll get the press conference set up for an hour from now. In the main conference room. Remember, I'd like it to be as short and sweet as possible. The last thing I want to do is stir up mass hysteria about a serial killer."

"We agree, Chief. And the last thing we want is a serial killer or abductor, if there is one, to get another victim. Two is more than enough."

"We can all agree on that. OK, see you two in an hour."

Ginny used part of the hour to call Newman's ex-wife,

and then Franley at the school, to tell them about Newman's body and the upcoming press conference. Neither of them was able to provide Ginny with any new information.

The press conference began five minutes late. The usual dozen or so press and TV reporters, along with their cameramen and technicians, were squeezed into the conference room. The chief made a few introductory remarks, then turned things over to Ginny.

Ginny dryly described the finding of Newman's body. She did not make any reference to Amy Richardson, nor the possibility that these two missing persons were in any way linked.

Ginny's answer to virtually every question was, "Sorry, but this investigation is just getting underway. We have nothing to add at this time." The desired result occurred; the conference ended twenty minutes after it had begun.

Ginny and Caruso arranged for one of the detectives — who was going out for a late lunch — to bring back sandwiches for them. They spent a good part of the afternoon checking various databases and learning all that they could about the two fisherman who had found Newman's body. They had no police records and were considered solid, dependable employees by their employer.

Late in the afternoon, CSI reported that they hadn't found anything else at the lake, especially not any indication of another body being dumped there. They had gathered seven good tire molds, but it would be the next day before any information about the tires and possible associated vehicles was available. They also reported that the victim's cellphone had been turned over to IT, but they were sure there'd be no news until the next day at the earliest.

Ginny and Caruso called it a day, both heading home frustrated by the day's events and worried about making some real progress before the serial-whatever struck again, either with Amy or a new victim.

While driving home, Ginny got a phone call from Mary Beth. The realtor and her firm's staging expert had toured Ginny's condo. Ginny was relieved to hear that their recommendations were all minor and, in fact, almost identical to those made by the second realtor interviewed: remove the recliner so the living room would look larger; remove some of Ginny's clothes from the closets in order to de-emphasize the limited closet space; and remove some of the photographs on the walls and shelves to depersonalize the space. Ginny authorized Mary Beth to arrange for the recliner to be donated to the Salvation Army or Goodwill.

That evening, Joe and Ginny spoke on the phone for about 15 minutes. Joe was set to tell Ginny all the details of his first day on the task force, but he only had a chance to give her a two-minute summary. They spent the rest of the call talking about Ginny's case, the discovery of Newman's body and what it might mean for Amy or a third victim-to-be. Joe tried to comfort Ginny as best he could, but she remained frustrated and worried.

Chapter 19

The next morning, Ginny and Caruso were again going through their notes together, hoping to come across something they missed earlier. Until they did, they were clueless as to what to do next.

"Excuse me," said Ginny as she reached for and picked up her ringing phone. "Hello, Detective Harris."

"Hi, Ginny," said the easily recognized medical examiner. "You might want to swing by. I found something I think you'll find interesting."

"OK, Doc, we'll be there in a few."

Fifteen minutes later, Ginny, Caruso and the medical examiner were standing next to Newman's body, laid out on a steel table.

"OK Doc, you obviously got our attention. What is it?"

The medical examiner pulled down the sheet covering Newman. Picking up one of Newman's arms, the medical examiner pointed to a number of long, thin cuts as well as what looked to be burns made with a cigarette. He then pointed to Newman's fingers, three of which were bent in such an abnormal way that there was no question to their being broken. And broken in more than one place.

"Torture?" asked Caruso.

"Can't think of any other cause. Clearly not accidental. And, whereas the cuts and burns could have been self-inflicted, that's very unlikely, and, in fact, damn near impossible for the broken fingers."

"Well, that sure puts a new slant on things. Why was he tortured?" asked Ginny. "For information? Or revenge?"

"Or maybe just a random psychopathic thrill seeker," added Caruso.

"I'll leave you detectives to figure out the who and the why. My job is to just show you the what."

"That you did, Doc," said Ginny. "Thanks."

"My pleasure. Oh, and by the way, no defensive wounds, or skin under his fingernails."

Back at headquarters, with Ginny at her desk and Caruso at Joe's, the two detectives tried to fully grasp what they had just learned.

"OK," said Ginny. "This points to a few new directions. To state the obvious, torture makes it extremely unlikely that Newman was selected at random, or killed just because he was in the wrong place at the wrong time."

"True. Unless it actually is a psychopath."

"Agreed. But if it's not, then Newman was picked up and tortured either to get some information he had or to take revenge for something he had done — or hadn't done, but should have."

"Yup. Either way, we gotta dig a lot deeper into the life and times of one Howard Newman."

"Exactly. Denny, let's first check with CSI. See if they learned anything from all those tire track molds they made by the lake. Then we oughta brief the chief."

"Agreed."

A phone call with CSI was relatively disappointing. "We

were able to make seven molds. Not bad, if I do say so myself, given how frozen most of the ground was. Of the seven molds, we were able to identify three specific tires. Unfortunately, all three are common original equipment on multiple common vehicles, two of the tires being for pickups and one for cars. These three, plus two of the other four molds, could be used to confirm an exact match if and when a tire or another mold is brought in. The final two molds weren't clear enough to identify a tire, or likely to be usable to confirm a match."

"Well, that's better than nothing," said Ginny.

"Sorry we couldn't come up with anything more definitive."

"At least it might confirm a suspect once we have his tires. Thanks again."

Ginny and Caruso then brought the chief up to date.

"Thanks, guys. Sorry he was tortured, but that at least gives you a few more possibilities to explore. We gotta find something, before this bum acts again and we either find Amy's body or another person goes missing."

"We know, Chief. We know. We're doing all we can."

"I know. Just try to do more."

"Uh. Yeah, sure," said Ginny as she and Caruso left the chief's office and returned to their desks.

///////////

First thing that same Tuesday morning, Joe stopped in to see if Deputy Sheriff Graham had a few minutes for him.

"Sure thing, Joe. Come on in and close the door. Grab a seat."

"Thanks, Larry," said Joe as he went in, closed the door and sat down. "This won't take long."

"Not a problem. For what can I do you?"

"It's about that motel I'm staying in."

"Uh oh. I know it's not a four-star place, but… What is it? Bed bugs? Noise? Or what?"

"No, no. It's not that at all. It's just a bit constraining. I mean, for a few days it's totally fine. But, as this assignment will last several months, I'd like to find a bigger place, with at least a small kitchen. Most likely, a small apartment."

"Fully understand. Hell, that's exactly what I'd do if I were in your shoes."

"Fantastic. How do I go about it?"

"Pretty straight forward. First, you can spend as much as you'd like on rent, but we can only reimburse you for up to what the motel is costing."

"Makes sense. How much is that?"

"Let's see," said Graham. After a few clicks on his computer, he continued, "So, that's just about $2,100 a month, including utilities, TV cable and a phone."

"Great. That'll help me narrow down my search. Any suggestions where to start?"

"Sure do. And you're in luck. You'll be spending time later in the week with Gretchen. Although she's officially my admin assistant, she, in fact, really runs this place. She knows this town and darn near everyone in it. Real well. She'll be a super help with your apartment search."

"Great. I appreciate that. Sounds like she's the right one."

Graham called Werner to his office and solicited her help in finding a rental unit for Joe. After a few minutes discussing price and Joe's wishes as to size, number of rooms, maximum distance from the office and so on, Gretchen said, "Shouldn't be a problem. Joe, give me a day or two to see what's out there. We should be able to put together a few options for you by the time we start working together on Thursday."

"Great. Thanks, Gretchen. I appreciate your help. See you on Thursday. And thank you also, Larry."

Joe spent the rest of the day working with Helen Radoff, the Human Resources supervisor, and Karla Simmons, the clerk reporting to her. Joe was surprised that the two of them were able to handle all the personnel matters for the sheriff's office as well as the county and DEA task forces. He soon realized this was possible only because they were primarily focused on clerical matters. Interviewing, hiring and personnel problems were handled by the sheriff or deputy sheriff and the group heads in the two task forces.

This was, however, the perfect spot for Joe to learn about each of the task force members. With Radoff's approval, Simmons shared the personnel files for all the task force members with Joe, and even the files for previous task force members who had left within the past year. Despite not having access to the personnel files of the part-time members of the task force, this offered Joe a wealth of information. Joe made notes about each full-time task force member — how long they had been on the task force, the date or dates of each position they'd filled on the task force, where they worked prior to the task force and any commendations or black marks on their record.

If I can find out when each of the corrupt practices was believed to have started, I might be able to eliminate some of these folks as possible suspects.

/////////////

Ginny was happy to be back at Joe's house that Tuesday evening. She hoped Joe would be able to call so that they could discuss her case in detail. Ginny was confident that Joe would have some good next steps for her and Caruso to pursue.

Joe called a few minutes before 8:15.

With all the patience she could muster, Ginny first listened to Joe describe his day.

Finally, it was Ginny's turn to talk about her case. As Ginny began bringing Joe up to date, she started pacing back and forth in front of the kitchen counter. "Joe, we're really struggling with this one. Every area we check leads to a dead end. We're out of ideas. And I — in fact, both of us — are scared shitless that Amy's body will be found, or another person will go missing. It's like we're just sitting around waiting for the next bomb to drop."

"Calm down, Ginny. I get that you're nervous and frustrated. But those feelings won't do anything to help you solve the case."

"I know, but…"

"The one potentially useful new piece of information is that the teacher was tortured. There has to be something he knew or did to cause that. You need to do a really deep dive into his past. And his activities just before his disappearance. Sure, it could be a psycho nut who did this for no reason, but that's unlikely, and also a theory that, at this point, is tough to follow up on. So, I think you have to try to uncover the reason for the torture. That very well could lead you to who the torturer is."

"Can't argue with that. Not something Caruso and I haven't thought of, but I feel better talking it through with you."

"I understand."

"Joe, any thoughts about the link between Newman and Amy, the girl missing from that school?"

"No special insight. Other than they were both at the same school, and he was her teacher last year. Was there a relationship more personal than teacher-student? Did they both see or learn something? And so on. Definitely worth pursuing the possibilities. And now having his cellphone might produce some useful information."

"OK, thanks for your input."

"Hang in there, Ginny. I'm sure you and Caruso will break through this at some point."

"Yeah, but let's hope it's before we have another death or disappearance."

"Amen to that."

Ginny spent a solid two hours tossing and turning in bed before she finally fell asleep. Her rehashing the two cases she and Caruso were struggling with soon turned to her focusing on her relationship with Joe. *I love and miss him so much. Not just personally, but also profession-ally. I can't wait to talk with him about our case. Even if he doesn't have great new suggestions, just talking it through with him helps. Damn, I was never like this with anyone else before. I was always my own person. Now it's like I'm waiting for suggestions from Joe. Or feeling better about my own lack of new ideas when Joe admits he doesn't have any new ideas either. I never had these feelings, or maybe just didn't realize it, when he and I were working all our cases together.*

Chapter 20

Joe spent all day Wednesday following the accounts payable clerk around. Most of her work was the routine payment of bills, for the sheriff's office as well as the two task forces. She followed a clear set of rules as to whether the dollar amount required one or two signatures to approve a payment and what level person had to be the signer or signers of the check.

Joe focused on the type of payment he was most interested in. Namely, one or more task force members obtaining cash for a drug buy. Joe was not surprised to see that only used bills, not in serial-number sequence, were used. There was some type of optical reader that recorded all the serial numbers when a stack of bills was fed through the unit. This, of course, was extremely useful in having objective evidence of how the money moved from the undercover agent to the drug seller to whomever. Joe asked how they kept track of the money used and compared it to how much they might get back when they later made a drug bust. But the clerk was only able to explain the front part of the process — getting the money for the buy — that she was involved in.

Chapter 21

Joe spent Thursday and Friday with Gretchen Werner. Joe found these to be a very informative couple of days. Werner's responsibilities gave her involvement in and oversight of many of the processes of interest to Joe: how funds used for an undercover drug buy are requested and approved, tracked and (hopefully) eventually recouped; how seized drugs are physically transported, weighed and stored, and the paperwork following these steps; how warrants are requested and approved; and how suspects are jailed, interviewed and eventually indicted and tried. Werner had worked in the sheriff's office for more than fifteen years and was extremely knowledgeable about all these processes and procedures. In fact, she had developed many of them.

"Gretchen, you must really be an expert in administration."

"Well, I have been doing it for a long time. But why do you say that?"

"Just look at your title: administrative assistant to the head of Administration. Administration isn't your middle name, but it clearly is your first and last."

After a chuckle, Werner replied, "Yes, but don't get too carried away by titles of people or departments. We all tend to jump in and do a lot of things. Anything that needs to get done, regardless of one's title. And, by the way, my middle name is Ellyse."

"Nice name. Thanks for sharing that little secret with me. Now can we switch topics and talk about undercover drug buys?"

"Sure. What do you want to know?"

"Pretty much everything. But, mostly about the money for the buy and then the handling of the drugs once they're purchased."

"OK. Here goes. Interrupt me with questions whenever you want. First off, one of the undercover agents sets up a buy. This doesn't come as a shock to anyone since it was probably several weeks in the making."

"But how do the people here in the office find out?"

"There's a weekly meeting of the so-called policy board. It assists RAC Singleton in managing the task force. It's sort of like a board of directors of a company. It's made up of high-level officers from a few of the various police departments and sheriff's offices, and from the Ohio BCI. Plus, of course, Singleton, representatives from the prosecutor's office and a few state and federal agencies, and the heads of the various task force departments. The board sets the overall objectives of the task force, establishes priorities on what to focus on and then reviews accomplishments vs. the objectives."

"Oh? This is the first I've heard of this policy board."

"The first thing to point out is that it really has little to do with policy, whatever that is. Its main purpose is to ensure that all the groups involved know what's going on. And, as I said, when needed it also sets priorities."

"Priorities? Like what?"

"All types. Let's say there's three possible buys trying to be set up, but we can only get enough cash for two. This group decides which two. Or if there are competing demands for air surveillance, or for highway interdiction activities, this group decides which one to pursue. Or at least to pursue first."

"Sounds like a pretty important weekly meeting."

"It is. Of course, more important some weeks than others. I'm the secretary of the board, so I arrange the meetings, prepare the agendas, take meeting notes and so on."

"Got it. OK, let's get back to the drug buy. So, the buy's set up, and say the agent needs 50 grand next Tuesday."

"Once the policy board approves that specific buy, and puts a dollar cap on it, let's say $100,000, I can approve the agent's request for the $50,000. I arrange for accounts payable to get the money delivered here a day or two before it's needed. We count it numerous times, scan and electronically record all the serial numbers and then store the cash in Deputy Graham's safe."

"And then?"

"On the day of the buy, we get it to the undercover agent, usually meeting him (it's almost never a her) in some pre-arranged location. Although sometimes skipped when time is tight, the undercover agent should count the money one more time before signing the receipt for it. Even if they don't count it, their signature makes them liable for the whole $50,000."

"I'd sure count it if it were me."

"Me too, but…"

"OK, so the agent presumably meets with the bad guys and buys the drugs. Then what?"

"The agent needs to turn in all the drugs. He also has to do an accounting that ties together the $50,000, the price for the drugs and the amount of drugs purchased and turned in."

"How's all that verified?"

"Pretty sharp. You've already identified the first big hole in our system. We can't tell if the price reported is the actual price. So, to make up an extreme example, if the agent reported a price twice as high as the actual price, he could keep half the cash. Or he could buy twice as much drugs and turn in only half."

"And you'd never know?"

"Sometimes not. But we get pretty good hints. First off, we have a good idea of the going price for a given drug of a given strength and quality. Also, if we arrest the dealer and they talk, they'll often mention the amount of drugs or the price. Can't always believe what a dealer says, but if this kind of discrepancy happens repeatedly with under-cover agent X, there's a pretty good chance agent X is skimming some of the money — or some of the drugs — for his own use or resale."

"Wow. How often is X caught?"

"Not very often. Suspicion is easy, but hard evidence is a lot tougher to get. First off, my example of the agent reporting a price double the actual price is unrealistic. They're more likely to inflate the price by only 10% or so. This still leaves them with a bunch of money or valuable product in their pockets, and the ten percent price discrepancy is almost impossible to detect."

"And you'd never know?"

"Sometimes not."

"That's too bad."

"It is. Of course, corrupt agents have to be careful how and where they spend their found money. We notice if an agent is living way above what he can afford on his salary. And, if he keeps some of the cash, remember, we know all the serial numbers."

"How about when the drug trafficker is caught?"

"They may talk, but they're known liars. Why should we believe what they say about the amount of drugs or the price involved in the undercover buy? As I said, we get suspicious when differences keep arising with regard to one or two agents, but we can't get much beyond suspicions."

"We're not doing anyone any favors when we tempt officers with how easy this could be."

"Couldn't agree more. But not sure how to close the loopholes. Oh, and there's one more."

"Go for it."

"When we conduct a drug bust and collect drugs or piles of cash. Or both."

"And?"

"Depending on how many agents are in on the bust, and whether or not they're all in on the cheating, it's real easy to underreport the amount of drugs and money seized."

"OK, but that would probably require two or more to be in on it."

"True. But remember, many of our members have worked together for years, so it's not inconceivable."

"One more question. Once the seized drugs are stored in the sheriff's evidence locker and the seized cash in Deputy Graham's safe, how easy is it for someone to steal some of the seized property?"

"We think pretty hard, but maybe we just haven't caught anyone at it yet. The drugs and money are recounted and signed off on every time they're moved or transferred from one person to the next."

"Gretchen, this has been super helpful. Thanks for putting up with all my stupid questions."

"Joe, your questions weren't stupid at all. But if you're all done, let's break for lunch. After lunch, we can go through some of our procedures and, of course, the all-important forms associated with them. Then, after that, I want to review some photos and descriptions of possible apartments with you."

And that's what Joe and Gretchen did: lunch, followed by a review of several task force procedures and forms.

Joe found the information on asset forfeitures to be among the most interesting. Unlike "innocent until proven guilty" which applies almost everywhere in the American criminal justice system, civil asset forfeiture allows the government to seize cash, cars, real estate and other property suspected of being connected to criminal activity, even if the owner is never charged, arrested or convicted. With court approval, forfeiture of the seized assets takes place. Forfeited assets are then usually shared among the state and local law enforcement agencies that participated in the seizure. This sharing is based on the relative value provided by each participating non-federal agency.

"Joe, I'm sure you'll wind up preparing TDF forms for seizures you participate in. Your objective, using puff but not lies, is to make your role sound as important as possible, thereby increasing the proportion of seized assets that are given to your home agency. So your policing skills and creative writing abilities are both important."

"Yeah, I'm aware of this, mostly from my time with the Chicago PD. But it seems to have become much more of a competitive sport since then."

"You bet. Think tight budgets might play a role in this?" asked Werner with a smile.

"Thanks for the info on procedures, especially the asset forfeiture one."

"My pleasure."

Joe and Werner then spent the last half-hour or so on Thursday afternoon reviewing descriptions and photos of five possible rentals that Werner had selected. Based on descriptions, locations and photographs, Werner had weaned the list down from 10 to five. She and Joe further narrowed the list to three, and Werner said she'd try to arrange for Joe and her to visit the selected three the next day.

Friday morning, Joe was especially pleased to have been allowed to observe one of the weekly policy board meetings. He paid close attention when the discussion focused on the next week's plans, including an upcoming buy as well as a series of "knock & talks" with known traffickers in the area. *Hope I can get directly involved with that buy, and a few of the knock & talks.*

Just before lunch, Joe and Werner headed out to see the three selected rental possibilities. After a quick lunch at Taco Bell, they first visited a private house. The floor above the non-attached garage had been converted to a rental apartment. This was quickly eliminated when it became apparent the so-called kitchen was nothing more than a hot plate and a microwave. The second option visited, a two-bedroom garden apartment just off Lafayette Road, was an immediate hit: large rooms; a full kitchen; well-located; a price of $1450 per month for the fully-furnished unit; and the ability to rent month-to-month without a lengthy lease. Joe signed on immediately and gave the building manager a check for the first month's rent. Werner called and canceled their visit to the third possibility.

Joe thanked Werner repeatedly for all her help. Before leaving Medina for the weekend, he checked out of his hotel room. On the drive back to Jasper Creek, Joe was mentally developing a list of all he wanted to bring back on Monday for his new home away from home.

Chapter 22

The second half of Ginny's and Caruso's week served mainly to increase their frustrations and worries. They dug as deep as they could into Newman's past, going as far back as his high school years in Indiana. They found nothing out of the ordinary, and definitely nothing that might lead to his being tortured. Talking with some of his long-forgotten friends, old teachers and colleagues uncovered nothing of note. Neither did talking (in some cases for the second time) with several fellow teachers, past and current students and neighbors. The only link they could find between Newman and Amy was their teacher-student relationship, which was described by all as a closer-than-most student-teacher relationship, albeit a perfectly appropriate one. Even in a follow-up call with his ex-wife, she had nothing additional to say; he was just a "normal, OK" husband and they had had a "normal, OK" marriage.

But their call to IT yielded at least some useful information. Denny walked over and stood next to Ginny as she dialed and directed the call through her speakerphone. "Sorry, Guys, checking his cellphone showed no calls that seem at all suspicious. And his phone is one of the old ones, without GPS, so there's no history of where he's been."

"Damn."

"Hang on, Ginny. Let me finish. We also checked the

megadata on his home phone. And he received a call from a burner cell about a week after the girl went missing from that same school."

"Damn, again. I assume that burner is untraceable."

"You bet. One call and toss it. Totally untraceable."

"Too bad. But, hey, we appreciate you doing your magic on his phones so quickly." Ginny hung up and turned to Denny. "Jeez, his life seemed to be as close to a blank page as possible, except possibly for that burner call. There's nothing concrete to pursue, much less develop a theory around. Can't see any reason for him being tortured."

"Can't argue with that, Ginny. Should we take another shot at trying to learn more about Amy?"

"Sure. Why not? We've got nothing to lose, not to mention nothing else to investigate."

And so Ginny and Caruso returned to Pond View Girls Academy. They spent almost one and a half days talking, in several cases for the second time, with Amy's current and prior teachers, with members of the administration who had had anything to do with her over the past few years, and, of course, with several of her current and prior classmates, housemates and teachers.

Talking with Emily Felding, a girl rooming down the hall from Amy, they did uncover one fact. "On two of Amy's prior runaways, she was assisted by a boy — or, a man. The same one both times."

"Do you know his name?" asked Ginny.

"No. I never met him, and Amy would never talk about him."

"What did he look like?"

"No idea. He was always in his car and I couldn't really see his face."

"Do you know what model car it was? Did you get the license?"

"I was too far away to read the license plate. I'm pretty sure it was a green car. Maybe a Mazda."

"Did you see him when Amy went missing a couple of weeks ago?"

"No, it was the two times before. Both were times when Amy left, not when she came back."

"Anything else?" asked Caruso.

"I assume he was a secret boyfriend, but who knows? It could have just been a friend who happened to be male."

"Thanks, Emily. You've been very helpful. Here's my card. Please call me if you think of anything else."

Another talk with Amy's roommate, Carol Davis, also turned up a small, new tidbit.

"It was getting a bit sickening. Amy was always raving about Professor Newman. How smart he was. What a great teacher he was. How much he really cared about his students. She sounded like one of those love-torn teens, infatuated by an older man. I bet it relates to how cold and uncaring her father always was."

"Do you think they were having an affair?" asked Ginny.

"Oh, heavens no. Unless maybe just in her head. She did spend time with him in his office, but I'm sure it was all above board. She said she wished he was one of her teachers this year. Even though she was not interested in chemistry, she was thinking of taking Advanced Chemistry next year just to be in his class again."

"OK, thank you, Carol."

Chapter 23

Ginny couldn't wait for the weekend to arrive. She hoped that Joe would be able to make it home. *I really miss him. Much more than I thought I would. I, of course, want to hear all about what he's been up to. But, most of all, I need to tell him what I'm going through mentally, even if it gets him upset. I've got to figure out how to tell him where my head is at.*

Sure enough, Joe did make it home that weekend. But, as he participated in a late Friday night raid, he couldn't head home until Saturday morning. He left Medina early Saturday morning and arrived home while Ginny was still relaxing over her post-breakfast second cup of coffee.

Over fresh cups of coffee, Ginny got right into it. "Other than a few errands and perhaps a few extracurricular activities in the bedroom, I want us to spend most of this weekend talking to each other. I feel like we haven't really been together ever since you started on the task force."

"I know exactly what you mean. I feel the same way. Our brief phone calls don't do it, and the weekends here just seem to fly by."

"OK, it's a deal then."

"Yup. What're the list of discussion topics we need to get through?"

"It's a short list, but it might take a while to get through it all. First off, we've made some progress on trying to sell my condo, and we need to make a decision. Then I want to tell you all the details of where Denny and I are on our cases. And I want all the details on what you've been up to — what you did this past week, what conclusions you've reached or are considering, your next steps, etc. And then we need to be honest with each other."

"Huh? Whaddaya mean? I've never lied to you."

"I know, Joe. Me neither. But I've been thinking all kinds of things and we need to talk them all through."

"Yeah, sure. Just tell me, should I be worried?"

"I don't think so, but let's wait 'til we have the discussion."

"Sounds scary. But sure, we have to talk about it. Whatever it is."

"I'll start with the condo. This is probably the shortest topic to get through."

"Go for it. Let's just refill our coffee cups and get more comfortable in the living room."

As soon as they settled in next to each other on the living room couch, Ginny began. "Believe it or not, we have two offers, and a third couple may want to make an offer."

"Fantastic. I was afraid we'd be sitting out there for months with nothing."

"Me too."

"Gimme the details."

"The first offer is for $138,500. That's less than we're asking, but the offer is all cash, meaning there's no delay or contingency for the buyer to get a mortgage."

"It's on the low side, but fast and sure are nice pluses."

"The second offer is for $152,000, but it's contingent on them getting a satisfactory mortgage."

"Hmmm. How long could that delay it?"

"The realtor told me it could be a month or so. The realtor's pretty sure the couple will qualify for a mortgage, but, of course, it's not certain until it happens."

"And you said there might be a third offer?"

"Yeah, a couple have been back twice to look. They seem very interested, but no offer yet. Nor any idea of the amount if they were to make an offer."

"Which way are you leaning?"

"Towards the higher offer, even though it's contingent on a mortgage. It's a great price, and there seems to be a fair amount of interest in the place, so even if this offer falls through..."

"Works for me. I'm in with the $152k offer if you are."

"Deal. I'll call Mary Beth tomorrow, after we've had a chance to sleep on our decision."

They then spent the next ninety minutes or so talking police business. Ginny first filled Joe in on how she and Caruso learned that Amy seemed to have had a boyfriend who helped her on some — or all — of her earlier runaways, and that Amy felt extremely close to, maybe even having a crush on, Newman. Joe then described what he had been doing and learning on the task force.

"OK. A pee break, and then let's honestly dive into this dishonesty discussion."

"Joe, I —"

"I know. Sorry. I don't mean to make fun of it. I know it's something you feel strongly about, so I take it seriously."

Back from their break and with their coffee cups again refilled, Joe started. "OK, Ginny. What is it?"

"Joe, I don't know how to even start —"

"It's not another man, is it?"

"Joe! No way in hell! That's the last thing. It's not even remotely possible."

"OK, then. Just jump in and start telling me."

"You're right. Here goes. Please don't interrupt until I get it all out."

"I'll try not to."

"At first I thought it was a feeling of being trapped once I sold my condo and we had only one place. I'd no longer have my condo as my security blanket."

"Ginny, we had talked about —"

"Joe, you agreed not to interrupt."

"Oops, yes I did. Sorry."

"But it turns out it wasn't that. I'd had those feelings early on, but they kind of mostly evaporated."

"Good."

"But there's something else."

"Yes?"

"Until we started spending so much time apart 'cause of your task force assignment, I hadn't realized it. Joe, in a nutshell, I've become too dependent on you. I didn't realize it when we were always together, but I look to you to take the lead and make all the suggestions on everything."

"Ginny, I —"

"Joe! Let me finish. Please! You're clearly the more experienced and better detective, so, although we were equal partners, I basically fell into the role of junior detective. It wasn't anything you did or said, it was me acting unconsciously. And everyone in the department, whether you realize it or not, also views you as the senior member of our team. And then for all the other non-work stuff, it's like I love you too much. I know that must sound crazy, but I just automatically agree with almost everything you say or suggest. For years, I was fiercely independent, and worked my way up to detective all by myself. But since you and I, whatever, I'm now more an appendage of you rather than my own person."

"Ginny, how long have you been feeling this way?"

"I really don't know. Probably quite a while, but I didn't realize it when we were always together. It's only since you've been away, and I've been working with Caruso, where we're truly working as equals, or maybe I'm even a bit more senior than him, that I recognized it."

"So what are you saying, Ginny?"

"I don't know. Joe, I love you more than anything on earth. And I'd be devastated if we weren't together. But we have to somehow change something so I don't feel like I'm surrendering myself to you. Am I making any sense?"

"I think so. But I'm still trying to absorb and understand it. We just have to figure out what to do about it."

"Whew. Thanks for not blowing up at me, Joe. I was really worrying about how to tell you all this."

"You did just fine, Ginny. And remember, you can always tell me anything."

"Thanks. What say we pick this up tomorrow? I'm drained and ready for sleep."

"Works for me."

Chapter 24

Joe and Ginny both slept until almost nine the next morning. After a leisurely breakfast which Joe cooked, Joe asked Ginny if she was sure she wanted to sell her condo.

"Positive. In fact, I'm going to call Mary Beth this morning and tell her the condo offer we want to accept."

"Are you really sure?"

"Of course."

"OK. Just want to be sure you're sure. After our conversation last night, I thought you might want to postpone selling."

"No way. Like I said last night, I'm past being worried about us having only one place to live. And however we figure out how to solve the other problem, the answer can't be not getting married or not living together."

"Glad to hear that. I gotta admit — I was totally spooked after last night's discussion. I'm glad those solutions are off the table."

"Off the table, ripped, burned and tossed into the trash."

"Perfect."

Ginny picked up the phone, called Mary Beth and informed her of the condo offer they wanted to go with.

Mary Beth agreed with their choice and promised to keep them up to date as things developed, hopefully leading to a reasonably quick closing within the next several weeks.

Joe and Ginny then settled back on the living room couch to continue the discussion from the night before.

"OK, Ginny, so what do we have to do to solve the problem? What do we call it, by the way? Your lack of independence?"

"It's sorta that. But not exactly. Why don't we just call it 'the problem'?"

"Works for me. But we still have the question of how we solve the problem."

"It's pretty simple, short-term."

"Oh?"

"You're away most of the time as long as you're on the task force. I suggest, unless something important comes up, we don't talk during the week. That'll allow me plenty of opportunity to spread my wings, or prove things to myself, whatever, as I work with Denny. Hopefully, we'll still see each other most every weekend. When we review our work with each other during the weekends, we should try to avoid you giving me too much advice. It'll be more like just bringing each other up to date."

"And when my task force assignment is over?"

"I don't know. We may have to come up with a different solution. But there's also a decent chance that, as I re-prove myself to me while you're away, my confidence or self-esteem or whatever the hell it is comes back and the problem goes away."

"I sure hope it does, Ginny. I love you so much. I want our lives to be perfect together."

"Me too, Joe."

"In any event, I think we have our plan for as long as

I'm on the task force. I'll miss talking with you almost every night, but it's a small price to pay if it solves the problem."

"OK. We're set for now. Thanks for being so under-standing, Joe."

"Not sure I fully understand it, but, as we say in Spanish, 'Tu problem es mi problem,' or something like that."

Ginny leaned over and gave Joe a big hug, totally failing at trying to hide her tears.

Chapter 25

Joe was back at work early that next Monday.

"OK, Joe," said Graham, "time to get you out into the real world."

"Super. I'm ready to go."

"One thing first."

"Oh, what's that?"

"You need to swing into Youngstown and see RAC Singleton."

"Uh, oh. Am I in trouble already?"

"No, not at all. Singleton was going to be here this morning, but he got sucked into a bunch of meetings at the DEA office."

"Why do I need to see him today?"

"You need to get sworn in as a federal officer before you go out in the field."

"I knew that was part of the plan, but why is it so urgent?"

"Depending on the crime you're working on, and the specific arrangement with the perp or suspect, you need to be able to choose your state or federal credentials based on which make sense."

"For example?"

"Well, certain drug crimes are federal crimes and certain are state, so you clearly need to make an arrest with the right creds. But that's the straightforward part."

"Oh?"

"Yeah. Many drug crimes can be charged under either federal or state statutes."

"So how do we decide when to use which one?"

"It often depends on leverage."

"Leverage?"

"You heard me. Federal sentencing, and its schedule of minimum sentences, is significantly longer than state sentences. Especially if the suspect is caught with an unregistered gun. So it's often fairly easy to get your suspect to flip. 'Would you rather be charged with a federal crime, or would you prefer to give me the name of your supplier, or boss or customer, as the case may be, and be charged under more lenient state statutes?' Not surprisingly, flipping to get a state charge is chosen at least three-quarters of the time."

"Pretty slick."

"We gotta use all the tools that we can."

"Understood."

///////////////

Joe was back from his meeting with Singleton, along with his new federal credentials and shiny badge, just in time for lunch. Graham brought in sandwiches and arranged for Joe and John Turner, head of the task force's Highway Interdiction group, to have lunch together in a small office, just large enough for a little square table and four uncomfortable chairs.

"Hi, Joe. Good to see you again after our brief hello when you were introduced to all of us on day one."

"Likewise."

"After lunch you'll be heading out for a ten-hour shift

on Interstate 80. This first day, we'll have Deputy Sheriff Evans riding with you. He's been doing this for more than five years and knows it inside-out."

"Super. Sounds like a great way for me to learn the ropes."

"Yup. And while you're learning, let's pull a couple of dirt bags off the road at the same time."

"Works for me. So how do we decide who looks like they're hauling drugs?"

"Most often, we don't decide. We get leads from a bunch of other agencies, from the FBI, the DEA and Customs on the federal side and from state and local law enforcement folks."

"That makes sense."

"Other times, a potential perp just looks suspicious. Driving very carefully and always five miles below the speed limit, or a rusty old pickup truck able to accelerate like a Ferrari. Sometimes we just have a gut feeling and can't even say why."

"Got it. So, we pull them over and search their vehicle?"

"Afraid not. We can't do any profiling. That's a big no-no these days. Unless we have a solid lead identifying the driver or vehicle quite specifically, we can only stop someone if they commit a violation."

"But what if they don't?"

"You'd be surprised, but that's rarely a problem. If you follow someone for twenty miles, which you often have to, you can be almost sure they'll commit some violation. And it can be a very minor one: two miles over the speed limit, not signaling a lane change, tailgating too closely and so on."

"Pretty sneaky."

"Yeah, but legal and not profiling."

"Should be fun and educational."

"And productive, we hope."

Twenty minutes later, Joe drove the dark blue Ram pickup out of the parking lot, with Frank Evans sitting at his side.

"Nice set of wheels, Frank. Yours?"

"Ha. I wish. No, it belongs to one of the state or local agencies participating in this task force. Got it and two others just like it in an assets forfeiture about 18 months ago."

"Not bad. Those asset forfeitures are like a trust fund for law enforcement agencies all over."

"No question. The one weird thing is that the DEA can't participate in the spoils."

"Huh?"

"That's right. Federal agencies aren't allowed to."

"That's really ironic."

"Yeah. Their task forces and partnering state and local agencies can, but the DEA itself can't. They've got top-notch people, but they're severely underfunded. That's why they're called what they are."

"What's that?"

"DEA — Don't Expect Anything."

"I've heard that, but until now I never really knew why."

"Good. You've already learned something and we're not even on I-80 yet."

Joe turned right and was soon cruising at 70 miles per hour, going east on Interstate 80.

Ten minutes later, they heard over their radio that

another highway interdiction team had stopped a moving van about twenty miles behind them. With Evans' concurrence, Joe turned on the lights and siren, made a U-turn at the first Emergency-Vehicle-Only turnaround area across the median and was soon speeding west. Less than 20 minutes later, Joe pulled up behind the other task force vehicle and the stopped moving van.

Joe and Evans walked up to the rear of the moving van, where the two task force members were talking with the van driver and his passenger. Both the driver and passenger appeared to be in their mid-30s. But the physical similarities ended there. The driver was the stereotyped image of a trucker — tall, barrel chested, and overweight, with his beard reaching down to the second button of his red flannel shirt. The passenger was about five-foot-six, clean shaven and thin as a rail. He was dressed in jeans and boots, a heavy camouflage-colored jacket and an International Harvester cap.

Joe and Evans and Deputy Sheriffs Butler and Idelman nodded their hellos to each other. Joe and Evans listened to the discussion.

"I'll ask you again. Why'd you pull us over? We weren't doing anything wrong."

"Not according to my way of thinking."

"What'd we do?"

"Saw you change lanes without signaling. Twice."

"Fer crying out loud. What's the big deal? Nobody signals anymore."

"Well 4511.39 makes it an Ohio misdemeanor nonetheless."

"Boy, you guys oughta find something more useful to

work on. OK, write me my ticket so I can get out of here. We got a delivery to make."

"Afraid it's not that simple."

"Oh. And why's that?"

"We'd like to search your truck for illicit drugs."

"Don't you need a warrant for that?"

"Yes, we do. Unless you voluntarily consent to us conducting the search."

"And why would I do that?"

"For your own good."

"Oh? How's that?"

"Couple of ways. First off, without your voluntary consent, you and your vehicle will be stuck here for quite a while, probably three or four hours, while we get a search warrant."

"Jeez. That's like blackmail."

"Hang on. There's more. If we do find any drugs during our search, then things get interesting. We could charge you under either Ohio or Federal law. And, as I'm sure you know, Federal penalties are a lot stiffer than Ohio's. Now pay attention, here comes the important part. We tend to use Ohio law for those who are cooperative, and Federal law for the others. And, in this situation, you giving your voluntary consent for us to conduct the search is pretty much the definition of cooperation. Is that clear? Any questions?"

"Damn! It's blackmail."

"Call it whatever you wish. Now, do we or do we not have your voluntary consent to conduct a search?"

After a few seconds of mumbling under his breath, the

driver turned to his passenger and said, "Rocky, sounds like we got no choice. Better let them search."

"Yeah, it sucks. But it is what it is."

"OK, you can do the search."

"Good choice. Let me just have you sign here," said one of the agents as he held out a form on a clipboard and a pen to the driver. "This way, you can't later deny that you consented."

Once the form was signed, Joe remained behind the moving truck with the two suspects, while the other three agents climbed into the back of the half-loaded truck and began their search. Since the only thing in the truck were sealed moving-company boxes, the search took quite a while as the agents had to cut open and search each of the boxes. Sure enough, four of the approximately 50 boxes were half-filled with drugs in clear plastic bags.

Evans radioed for a tow truck to come to the scene and tow the truck with its contents to the sheriff's office. Joe and Evans arrested the two suspects, cuffed them, put them in the back of their car and drove them to the sheriff's office. The two other agents remained at the scene awaiting the tow truck.

"So, what happens next?" asked Joe.

"When we get to the sheriff's office, we'll process these two and put them in a holding cell. Once the tow truck starts towing the van here, Butler and Idelman will follow it in, then unload the drugs with our help, and have them identified and counted or weighed. The drugs then go into the evidence room. Then we're all back on the highway, continuing our shift."

"Glad I got to see that on day one. Was a good education."

"Happy to hear it."

"Yeah, I learned a lot. Thanks, Frank." *There's clearly plenty of opportunity for Butler and Idelman, or both, to stuff some drugs into their car. Surely before the tow truck gets here, and possibly afterward. Super easy if they're doing it together. Harder, but far from impossible, if only one of them is crooked.*

Back in his apartment that evening, Joe made detailed notes of the interdiction he participated in earlier that day, noting in particular the ways that Butler and/or Idelman could have skimmed some of the seized drugs before they were safely stored in the evidence room. *Definitely an insightful day. I'd love to call Ginny and fill her in. But I need to stick to our plan. I can tell her when I'm home this weekend.*

Chapter 26

*T*wo more days with the Highway Interdiction Group gave Joe four more opportunities to participate in stops, as well as a chance to work with a few more of the task force members. The one additional thing he learned was how much easier it was to steal when large amounts of cash were seized either along with or instead of drugs. The cash was much smaller physically, and it would be almost impossible to prevent one, or two, officers sticking a valuable stack of bills under his car seat or under something in the trunk of his car. Of course, if the money came from an undercover drug buy, the task force having recorded all the serial numbers made spending or depositing the money a less-than-simple endeavor.

Chapter 27

It was a discussion with Joe over the past weekend that led to a useful path for Ginny and Caruso. Following this path, good news arrived just before noon on Tuesday.

"OK, Denny, we got it."

Having obtained a search warrant the morning before, Ginny and Caruso had requested the metadata records of Amy's cellphone records for the past two years. Conversations and text message contents weren't provided, but the date of each call or text, whether it was an incoming or outgoing transmission, and the duration of each call or the text message's length were provided. The phone number called or texted — or from which Amy received a call or text — was also noted.

"Great. Given the amount of data, it'll take us some time, but this may very well lead us to the boyfriend."

"Yup. I can't wait to dive in. I'll ask Vern to bring back lunch for us so we can start right away."

"Sounds good to me. I'll meet you in the conference room. I need a quick pit stop."

Ten minutes later, Ginny and Caruso had commandeered the conference room. Ginny had written on the board the five dates of Amy's various runaways, and Caruso was sorting the piles of paper to separate out those dealing with the periods up to two months before and two months after each runaway.

"OK Ginny, here're two piles for you. I'll take two others. The first one finished wins the prize and gets to go through pile number five."

"Not exactly a huge incentive to work fast, but I guess it'll have to do," said Ginny with a smile.

The work was boring but rather straightforward. They were looking for phone numbers that had an increased number of calls or texts associated with them in the periods immediately before (and possibly after) each runaway. The theory was that Amy and her boyfriend would have been in more frequent contact, talking about and planning the runaway.

"In fact," added Ginny, "there probably would then be a large drop in transmissions with the boyfriend, maybe even radio silence, during the actual time Amy was gone. Assuming they were off someplace together, there'd be no need for them to be calling or texting each other."

It was after eight before Ginny and Caruso called it quits for the day. Earlier, Ginny had texted Joe to let him know that she'd be home late just in case he tried calling her that night.

"Denny, don't forget to wear your Sunday best tomorrow. We've got Newman's funeral at 10."

"Got it. I'm even going to shower in the morning. See you tomorrow."

"Night."

Chapter 28

The next morning, Ginny and Caruso were back in the conference room before 7:30.

"You're as bad as I am, Ginny. Why you here so early?"

"I just love the coffee here so much. Couldn't wait any longer for my first cup."

"Sure. And I bet getting back to these phone records has nothing to do with it."

"Well, yeah. OK. That's another good reason I came in early."

Caruso finished first so he started in on the data associated with Amy's most recent runaway.

Once Ginny finished, she said, "OK, done. While you're finishing the last pile, I'm going to start identifying some of the more frequent phone numbers."

"Go for it."

With access to databases not legally available to the general public, Ginny was able to associate a name and address with each of the phone numbers she selected. Starting with the most frequent numbers, Ginny soon identified Amy's calls with her parents, texts and occasional calls with her roommate and a few other students, and the local pizza parlor, Chinese restaurant and dry cleaner. Caruso joined in this effort as soon as he finished going through the last stack of papers.

At 9:15, Ginny and Denny took a break from what

they were doing and headed to the church for Newman's funeral. It took place in a depressing, flower-free chapel. The service, with a closed coffin, was led by a pastor who clearly didn't know Newman. Several colleagues and staff from the school, probably two dozen students from Newman's current and previous classes and a few neighbors attended. No relatives, not even his ex-wife, were in attendance. The service was fairly short, with eulogies by Franley and by two students. The two students, one from three years prior and one from the current year, praised Newman as one of their favorite and most effective teachers. Ginny and Denny remained for the entire service, but didn't notice anyone or anything out of the ordinary.

They were back at their desks by 10:45, heads again deep into the metadata from Amy's phone. "OK, we've identified most of Amy's regulars. Now let's focus in on those with the expected frequency increases before and possibly also after each of her runaways."

By noon, they had identified one number in particular that seemed to closely match the pattern they were looking for. While eating the pizza Detective Jones had brought back for them, Ginny began a search of various databases.

Ethan Thompson didn't have a large rap sheet, but neither was he a pure angel.

"Wow, that's a surprise," said Ginny. "Our boyfriend is 22, in fact almost 23. And Amy's what, 17? No idea how they even ever met. No major arrests or convictions, but he's been involved in a number of fights, not to mention one DUI. Seems like he never graduated high school.

Dropped out of Jasper High in the middle of his junior year."

"Not what I would have pictured as Amy's first choice. She's a bright, good student from a wealthy, or at least way-upper-middle class, family."

"How about we go have a chat with Mr. Thompson?"

"You bet. Let's go, Ginny."

"Two things first. We oughta update the chief, and I think we should swing by the school. Let's check if anyone there knows or has ever heard of him."

"Good points. We owe the chief an update anyhow, and it'll be nice to describe a little progress for once. Then, the more we know before we talk with Thompson the better. By the way, where do we find him?"

"He lives in an apartment on the southside, but he works at Pete's Pallets, over on 5th. Seems to be a small business that refurbishes old and broken pallets and then resells them. Presumably for a lot less than new pallets."

"I'm sure. Also sounds like the kind of work ideal for a high school dropout."

As expected, the chief was as quiet and noncommittal as usual. Nonetheless, he did seem pleased, or at least relieved, to learn of some progress in the case.

Ginny then drove to Pond View Academy. With organizing help from Mrs. Porter, the dean of students, Ginny and Caruso spoke one at a time with Amy's roommate and five of her friends. None of them recognized Thompson's name, or the photograph of him which Ginny had printed from the Department of Motor Vehicles' database of drivers' licenses.

They were soon on their way to Pete's Pallets.

Ginny parked directly in front. The facility was basically a small parking lot, totally contained by chain-link fencing, with a small shed in one of the rear corners. The lot was full of broken pallets, lumber, and three workbenches. Two or three men were at each of the workbenches. Despite the mid-30s temperature and remnants of snow still on the ground, they were coatless, most likely keeping warm by their physical labor.

Denny and Ginny immediately recognized Thompson at the closest workbench, but they wanted to introduce themselves to the manager first. They intentionally didn't stare at Thompson, but he eyed them with suspicion as they walked by.

Ginny and Caruso walked to the shed, knocked on the door and walked in. The shed was about twelve-feet square, one room with a couple of doorways in the rear, most likely one opening to a bathroom and the other a closet.

Caruso said hello to the man sitting at the desk. With no phone and very few papers on the desk, the man was either just resting or deep into a strategic planning session.

"You the manager?" asked Caruso.

"Yeah. Can I help you?"

Flashing his badge, Caruso continued, "Detectives Caruso and Harris. JCPD. We'd like to speak with one of your employees, Ethan Thompson."

"OK. Go ahead."

Ginny said, "Thanks," as she and Caruso left the shed and walked over to where Thompson was working.

"Ethan Thompson?" asked Caruso.

"Yeah."

"I'm Detective Caruso, and this is Detective Harris. We'd like to talk with you."

"What about?"

"Is there someplace we can go to talk?"

"Not that I know of. Ain't too many executive conference rooms here."

"How about we go sit in our car? At least it's warm, quiet and comfortable."

"OK."

The three of them walked to Ginny's car. Ginny got in the driver's seat, Thompson in the front passenger seat and Caruso in the back seat behind Ginny. Ginny turned the engine on and cranked up the heat.

"So, whaddaya wanna talk about?"

"Amy Richardson."

"What about her?"

"When did you last see her?"

"I dunno. A while ago."

"What's your relationship with her?" asked Caruso.

"Whatcha mean?"

"Are you relatives? Or friends? Or lovers? Or what?"

"Good question. I guess you could say we're good friends."

"How often do you two see each other?" asked Ginny.

"Varies."

"Can you be a little more specific?"

"Uh, yeah. I guess so. Probably every few months or so."

"And you call that good friends?" asked Caruso.

"Yeah. Well, we're both pretty busy. So we go for quality time together. You know, quality rather than quantity."

"Oh, I see," said Ginny. "And would those once every few months tend to be the times that she's run away for a few days?"

"Yeah, pretty much."

"Tell us more about those times."

"Not much to tell. Every once in a while, she gets all worked up about having to take all kinds of crap from everyone — her parents, her teachers, and most everyone else."

"And?"

"And she decides to get away for a few days without telling anyone when or where she's going. Makes her feel like she's back in control of her life."

"I see," said Ginny. "And where do you fit into all this?"

"She doesn't like to be alone. She likes me to go with her. We spend a lot of time talking and stuff."

"And stuff?" asked Caruso.

"Yeah, stuff. Like being together. And making out, and more stuff like that."

"How do you know when she's ready for one of these little trips? And how do you meet up?"

"She usually texts me. A couple of times she called instead of texting. We agree on the day and time, and I drive to a supermarket that's about ten blocks from her school. She walks to the supermarket, we meet up and head on out."

"Head on out to where?" asked Caruso.

"Depends."

"How about you elaborate a bit on that?"

"OK, sure. Sometimes we'll drive to a nearby town and settle into one of the cheap local motels. If it's not too snowy or too rainy, sometimes we go to one of the state parks and camp out. Like I said, it depends."

"How'd you two first meet?" asked Ginny.

"In some bar downtown. I don't even remember which one. I was legal, but she had to use fake ID to get served. Obviously, the bartender wasn't too thorough in screening for underage drinkers. But I had nothing to do with that."

"A bit surprising that you two got together. Given your age and all. You do know that she's only 17?" said Caruso.

"What? No way. She told me she was 18. I knew 'cause of her fake ID that she wasn't 21, but I was sure she was at least 18. If I'd known, we never would of, you know, uh, done some of the stuff we did."

"Not to worry. That's not why we're talking to you right now."

"So why are you?"

"We're trying to find Amy."

"Whaddaya mean? Where is she? Is she OK?"

"If we knew the answers to those questions, we wouldn't be trying to find her, now would we?" said Caruso.

"Uh, no, I guess not."

"Now it's our turn to ask you. Where is she?"

"How'd I know? I didn't even know she was missing until you just told me."

"Lying to the police is a crime, you know."

"I'm not lying."

"Right. You live and work here in Jasper Creek, but you never saw any of the newscasts or her mother's press conference or a newspaper article about her disappearance? And no one you know has spoken about it these past three weeks?"

"Well, I've been pretty busy."

"Ethan, you're digging yourself a hole that will get harder and harder for you to get out of. Many people a lot busier than you know about Amy's disappearance. And so do a lot of people even dumber than you."

"Hey, that's insulting."

"Very perceptive," said Caruso. "Maybe you're not quite as dumb as you seem."

"So, Mr. Thompson," said Ginny, "we need to know exactly when you last saw Amy."

"Gimme a minute. Lemme think. It was over a weekend, three or four weeks ago. Like normal, we met at that supermarket, then we went camping for the weekend, 'til I brought her back to the supermarket that Sunday afternoon."

"Where'd you go camping?"

"Near that Deer Valley State Park. We didn't actually go into the park or its campground. We just camped in the woods about a half-mile or so outside the state park. With a fire going and wearing the right clothes, camping in the winter is sort of neat."

"Did anyone see you that weekend?"

"Don't think so. Or at least we didn't see or speak to anyone. We like to camp in those kinda woods, where it's not likely that anyone else will camp there or even walk by. Especially in the winter."

"What time did you drop her off back at the supermarket that Sunday?" asked Ginny.

"Hmm. Don't know for sure, but probably between six and seven. Sky was just starting to get dark."

"And then what did you do?"

"Nuthin'. Went home, had dinner, watched some TV and went to sleep. Hadta be back here at work the next morning, you know."

"Mr. Thompson, would it be OK if we had our technicians search your car?"

"Sure. No problem. Whaddaya looking for?"

"Anything that might help us locate Amy. I'll call the station now and arrange for a couple of techs to come look at your car while you're still here at work. That way, it won't inconvenience you. May I have your car keys?"

"Here," said Thompson as he handed Ginny his car key. "It's the green Mazda over there," he added, pointing to one of the cars parked just outside the fence.

"One other thing. Could you describe, or even better, show us exactly where you camped?" asked Caruso.

"Think so. Might not be the exact spot, but I'm pretty sure I can get us pretty darn close."

"Great," said Caruso. "Let's plan on doing that as soon as our techs get here to check your car."

"OK, but you better clear it with my boss."

"Will do," said Caruso.

Thompson returned to work. Ginny called and requested two crime scene technicians to come check out Thompson's car. She also requested that an officer be sent to the Kroger supermarket where Thompson said he picked up and returned Amy and watch any video surveillance recordings to see if Amy and/or Thompson were recorded on the dates of her being picked up and returned. While Ginny was on the phone, Caruso walked back into the shack to tell the manager that they'd need to borrow Thompson for a couple of hours later that day to help them with a case they were working on.

An hour later, the two techs arrived. Ginny gave them the car key and explained what she hoped they'd find. Then Ginny, Caruso and Thompson left in Ginny's car.

Chapter 29

Ginny drove toward the state park entrance. Following Thompson's directions, she turned north onto a dirt road about a half-mile before the entrance. The dirt road ended a quarter mile later. Ginny turned off the engine, and the two detectives followed Thompson into the woods.

About 10 minutes later, Thompson pointed to a small open area ahead. "There. That's where we stayed."

"Are you sure?" asked Ginny.

"Positive."

The ground was covered with two or three inches of snow. There were many trees, but with all their leaves gone they offered little protection from the wind and blowing snow. The snow would have hidden any but very recent footprints.

Ginny and Caruso carefully walked around the area but found nothing. Ginny noted how the open space showed no signs of anyone walking, much less camping, there. There were no remnants of a campfire nor any broken branches.

"OK, that's it for now. We'll get you back to work now. Here are our cards. Please contact us if you think of anything else, or if Amy contacts you," said Ginny.

"And don't leave town without talking with us first," added Caruso.

"What? Why? Am I a suspect or something? Hell, you

don't even know what happened to Amy. Maybe nothing did."

"Let's say you're a person of interest for now. High interest, in fact. Not yet a suspect," said Caruso.

Ginny carefully marked the area and paid attention to how they had walked and driven. She wanted to be sure she could easily return to this exact site.

After dropping Thompson off at Pete's Pallets, Ginny said, "That site sure didn't look like anyone had been camping there. At least not for several months."

"I agree. But it wouldn't surprise me if their campsite was somewhere in that general area. He seemed to be taking us to where they had camped. Then, maybe at the last minute, he decided to throw us a curve."

"My thought exactly. Let's get Patrol to organize a search party to walk the entire area. Decent chance they might find something. I just hope to hell it's not a burial plot."

"Me too."

Ginny called the head of Patrol, filled him in on their thinking and requested that he assemble a search party, ideally as soon as possible so they could take advantage of the remaining daylight. She also described how to locate the spot Thompson had shown them.

Ginny and Caruso stopped for a quick lunch at a Burger King, after which they drove back to the dirt road they'd been on earlier with Thompson.

Around one-thirty, four patrolmen and seven firefighters, two paid and five volunteer, showed up. The fire chief took charge, laying out a grid pattern over an approximately two-square-mile area and assigning pairs of searchers to each section. He made sure each pair had a radio with which they could maintain contact with him. The fire chief remained by his car, making that the official command center.

About four hours later, as dusk was settling in, the fire chief called it quits for the day, recalling all the searchers back to his vehicle. He checked with each pair and noted on the map the areas that had been searched. He thanked everyone and made arrangements for the search to continue at eight the next morning.

Ginny and Caruso were disappointed but couldn't disagree with the fire chief's reasoning: Searching in the dark would have been dangerous and very likely unsuccessful. Ginny followed everyone else driving out. She dropped Caruso off at his car behind the station and headed home.

Chapter 30

The search was underway again by 8:30 the next morning. Many of the searchers were the same as those of the day before, but there were a few new faces, including four additional volunteer firefighters.

Just before eleven one of the search pairs radioed the fire chief, saying they thought they'd found something. The fire chief, Ginny and Caruso headed into the woods.

Sure enough, the area where the search pair was waiting had obviously been a campsite, including a section where there had been a campfire. About 20 yards away from the clearing, back in the woods, they found what looked to be a recently dug and refilled hole. The trees were so dense in this area that despite the lack of leaves, the solidly frozen ground was virtually snow-free.

"Oh, shit," said Ginny. "I don't want to even think what might be buried there."

"Well, we'll know soon enough," said the fire chief. Two of the volunteer firefighters went back to the fire truck and returned with shovels. Being very careful, the two firefighters began digging. It wasn't more than 10 minutes when one of the firefighters stopped digging and said, "Damn. A bone. And it looks human."

The fire chief halted the digging and ordered everyone to back up a good 50 feet. Caruso circled the whole area with crime-scene tape, while Ginny called the chief and reported their findings. The fire chief said he'd take care of getting the crime scene crew and the medical examiner notified. Caruso called Patrol and arranged to have a few uniformed officers report to the scene to protect the crime scene.

Less than an hour later, the place was jumping. More volunteer firefighters — as well as a few members of the public — had showed up, as had the crime scene technicians and the medical examiner and his crew. Plus, of course, several reporters and a few cameramen. Although a news helicopter was circling overhead, Ginny was pleased that little could be seen through the dense trees, despite most of the leaves being long gone.

By 2:00 PM, the medical examiner, with a large bag of bones and body parts in his van, was ready to head back to his office complex. The body had been cut into several large pieces. The head was all in one piece, and the torso was sufficiently intact to make it obvious that the victim was a female. One look at the face and Ginny and Caruso knew that it was Amy. Ginny took a photo of the face, being careful not to include the bloody severed neck in the photo. *Damn, it won't be fun showing this photo to Amy's parents for identification purposes.*

The crime scene technicians were still busy looking for any evidence, photographing everything and taking molds of several footprints, most of which were probably put there by the searchers.

Ginny and Caruso left, heading to the home of Amy's parents.

"Shit! I hate this more than just about anything else about this job," said Ginny.

"Me too. But we don't have any choice. I sure hope Mrs. Richardson isn't home alone."

"Yeah, it would be nice if her husband was there to give her some support. Especially at a time like this."

Sure enough, Mrs. Richardson was home alone. At Ginny's insistence, Mrs. Richardson called her husband at work and asked him to come right home. From the one side of the conversation they could hear, Ginny and Caruso realized that Mr. Richardson initially must have refused, agreeing to come home only after pleading and begging by his wife.

Ginny and Caruso hoped to wait until Mr. Richardson got home, but the awkward silence and intermittent questioning by Mrs. Richardson made that impossible.

"Mrs. Richardson, we had hoped to wait for your husband to arrive, but you obviously don't want us to. I'm afraid we have some very bad news."

Ginny could actually see the blood draining from Mrs. Richardson's face. "She's dead, isn't she?"

"Please sit down," said Caruso, as he gently held her by her shoulders and led her to the nearest chair.

"Yes, I'm afraid so," said Ginny. "We found her earlier today."

Ginny started to explain where and how they found Amy, but she quickly realized Mrs. Richardson was so shaken, and crying and screaming so loudly, that saying anything more would be a waste of effort.

Mr. Richardson arrived about 20 minutes later. Walking in and seeing his wife distraught in front of the two detectives, he immediately understood what was going on. "My God, is she dead? Tell me. You found her, didn't you? How? Where? Who's the bastard that killed her?"

"Mr. and Mrs. Richardson, please accept our sincerest condolences. We're so sorry," said Ginny. *God, I don't have any kids, but I can imagine what it must be like to learn that your teenage daughter has been murdered.* "Please rest assured that we, in fact the entire police force, are doing everything possible to determine who did this."

"Fine. But that won't bring Amy back."

"No. It won't."

Ginny then showed the photograph to the Richardsons. Ginny was sure that it was Amy, but she needed the identification to be made by a relative. Mr. Richardson nodded yes and turned away; Mrs. Richardson let out another scream.

Ginny and Caruso repeated their condolences, said they'd be in touch shortly, and left.

Driving away, Ginny said, "We didn't even stop for lunch today. And guess what, I'm not at all hungry."

"Not surprising."

Ginny called the station and learned that the video recordings from the supermarket did indeed show Amy being picked up by someone in a vehicle that looked like Thompson's. The date and time corresponded with what Thompson had told them. There was no record of her later being dropped off there. As the recordings were retained for only two months, there were no recordings related to any of Amy's earlier runaways. Ginny promised to swing by later to view the recording. Ginny then called the chief and brought him up to date. She explained that they were going to pick up the Thompson boy and bring him to the station for some serious questioning.

Ginny checked her notebook, noted Thompson's home address and she and Caruso headed there. Fifteen minutes later, Ginny pulled up in front of an older, rather rundown garden apartment house. It was one building, not a complex of buildings. The directory at the front door indicated there were about 20 residences. E. Thompson was handwritten on a slip of paper next to the button for apartment 3D. Ginny pushed the buzzer.

"Yeah?"

"Mr. Thompson. This is Detective Harris. We'd like to talk with you again."

"Jeez. Don't you ever give up? All I want is a little peace and quiet."

"We understand. But please let us in. We won't be staying long. I promise."

"Yeah. Yeah. Hang on."

Ginny opened the door when she heard the buzzer. She and Caruso walked up to the third floor and found Apartment 3D almost directly across from the stairwell.

Thompson's head was sticking out the partially open door. "This better be quick. You promised."

"Oh, don't worry. We'll keep our word," said Caruso as he eased the door all the way open. "Mr. Thompson, get your coat. We're going downtown for a few more questions."

"What? Why? I told you everything I know. I even took you to where Amy and I camped out."

"Coat! Now! Or would you rather we handcuff you and drag you off?"

"Hold on. No need. Lemme get my damn coat and turn off the TV."

"That's better," said Caruso as he followed Thompson into his apartment.

Ten minutes later, Thompson was in the back of Ginny's car and the three of them were on their way to the station.

"How'd you even know where I live?"

"Not too difficult for trained detectives like us," said Caruso. "Your having a driver's license makes it pretty simple."

"OK. But what do you want? I don't know any more than what I told you."

"We'll see about that," said Ginny. "We'll be at the station shortly."

Chapter 31

Ginny and Caruso let Thompson sit alone in the interrogation room for about 30 minutes. They found this time alone often irritated or worried suspects enough that they would say more than they had intended to. Ginny and Caruso used the time to run downstairs and view the video recording from the supermarket.

"Perfect, Denny. More proof if we need it. Amy's clearly visible."

"Yeah, and even though you can't see that Thompson's the driver, that clearly is a green Mazda."

Ginny and Caruso entered the interrogation room and sat down. Caruso placed the portable recorder on the table, told Thompson that the session would be recorded and turned the recorder on. He then recorded the date, location and names of the three people in the room and read Thompson his Miranda rights.

"Mr. Thompson," said Ginny, "we found where you and Amy had really camped. Wasn't too far from where you showed us, but you clearly were trying to send us down a dead-end alley."

"Not true. I showed you where I thought we had camped. Hell, how can I tell one tree from another?"

"Our technicians also found some damning evidence when they searched your car."

"Oh, yeah. What?"

"The tread pattern of your tires matched those found at your real camp site. And some of the dirt on the underside of your car clearly matches the dirt at the crime scene."

"Shouldn't be that big a surprise. I told you we went there in my car. And why'd you call it a crime scene?"

"'Cause that's what it is," said Caruso.

"Yeah? And what crime are you talking about? Amy running away?"

"You wish," said Ginny. "How about murder? We found the hole you dug."

"What murder? What hole? I don't know what you're talking about."

"Why'd you kill her, Ethan?" asked Ginny. "Was it an accident? And then you panicked and tried to hide her body and lie about everything? Or did you two have an argument and you lost your temper?"

"What? No! Why would I kill Amy? I liked her. And she liked me. A lot."

"Then we don't know why. How about you tell us?"

"I got a better idea. How about you get me a lawyer? I'm done talking 'til I got a lawyer."

"Probably the smartest move you've made in a while. Do you have an attorney you'd like to call? Or should we see about getting you a public defender?"

"I don't have no lawyer. And I couldn't afford him even if I had one. So I'll go for one of those promo bone lawyers that do the work for free."

"I think the term is pro bono," said Ginny. "Latin."

"Fine with me. I'm no redneck. I don't care if the lawyer's Latino or not."

"No," said Ginny. "Not Latino. I was saying that pro bono is a Latin term."

"Well. Thanks so much for the school lesson. Now we're done talking 'til my lawyer gets here."

Ginny went to fill the chief in, while Caruso went to his desk and called the County Prosecutor's Office. Walter Atley was the assistant prosecuting attorney on duty that evening. He agreed to arrange for the night-court judge to appoint a pro bono attorney, after which the attorney and Atley would walk over to the police station.

While waiting, Caruso walked two blocks to Kentucky Fried Chicken and brought back dinners for Ginny, Thompson and himself. It was close to eight that evening before Atley and Thompson's newly appointed pro bono attorney, Teresa Quill, arrived.

Introductions were made, Thompson and Quill spent about 15 minutes together while the others left the room, and then the interrogation session resumed.

About 25 minutes later, Caruso said, "So far, this has mostly been a repeat of what we discussed earlier before Thompson asked for an attorney. But we have three additional things to discuss.

"First, Ethan, why did you kill Howard Newman?"

Thompson blurted out, "What? Who? What are you talking about?" before his attorney was able to get him to stop talking.

"Detectives," said Quill, "my client clearly has no idea who or what you're talking about. Care to fill us in?"

"Happy to. But I don't think your client needs a briefing. He's well aware of this. Howard Newman is — or was — a chemistry teacher at Pond View. One of Amy's former teachers. He went missing and has since been found dead."

"And you think my client had something to do with this?"

"Sure do. Too much of a coincidence, given Amy's disappearance and death."

"I understand. But a little bit of evidence might be of value to your case."

"Right you are. And we're working on getting some. Secondly, Mr. Thompson, we're planning to arrest you tonight for the murder of Amy Richardson."

"What!" said Quill. "Isn't that a bit premature? Again, some real evidence might be appropriate."

"Well, you'll have your chance at the arraignment," said Atley.

"You guys must be under a lot of political heat to be acting like this," said Quill.

"Or perhaps our objective is to get a serial killer off the streets as soon as possible," said Ginny. "Oh, and by the way, our third point is that we'll be getting a search warrant for Mr. Thompson's apartment."

"Thanks for sharing all your exciting news with us. Ethan, don't worry. You'll have to spend a night or two in jail, but I'm confident you'll soon be out on bail. Or perhaps even released with no charges being filed."

And with that, the session ended. Quill left. Caruso took Thompson to get fingerprinted, photographed and otherwise processed for immediate arrest.

Atley and Ginny went to Ginny's desk. Ginny gave Atley the details needed for the search warrant request, and Atley arranged for the grand jury to hear Thompson's case Monday morning.

It was close to midnight when Ginny got to Joe's house. She got undressed and into bed, wishing that Joe was there to cuddle up next to her.

Chapter 32

Ginny didn't get to work until almost 8:30 the next morning. Caruso was already in the chief's office, bringing him up to date on the progress made the previous day. Just as Caruso was returning from the chief's office, the fax machine started clacking away. *Good for Atley. He already got the search warrant for Thompson's apartment.* Ginny arranged for two patrolmen and two crime scene technicians to meet Caruso and her at Thompson's apartment at 12:30. Ginny called Atley and thanked him for the quick turnaround on the warrant.

A little before 10, Ginny and Caruso left for Amy's funeral.

While driving, Caruso filled Ginny in on his update with the chief earlier that morning. "As usual, even as he was congratulating us for the progress we made, I couldn't help feeling —"

"No need to say it. I know the routine. Smile on his face, nice words coming out of his mouth, a pleasant handshake or hand on your shoulder, with his foot up your butt. All at the same time."

"Exactly. I couldn't have described it better."

"Yeah. Great job. Keep it up. But do more and do it faster."

"That's our chief."

"Sure is," said Ginny.

Upon arriving and entering the church, Ginny and Caruso couldn't help but compare this with Newman's funeral.

"Wow, Denny. This is quite a funeral. A zillion flowers, what must be a 20-person choir, and virtually all the seats occupied."

"A lot different than Newman's. This looks like all the students and most of the school's faculty and administration must be here."

"Very true. The only common element is that they're both closed coffins. For obvious reasons."

The pastor obviously knew Amy and her parents, and the eulogies from friends and family were nicely presented.

Ginny and Caruso offered their condolences to Amy's parents and said hello to several whom they recognized from the school.

Despite the favorable comparison to Newman's somber funeral, attending Amy's funeral was no more informative to Ginny and Caruso than had been Newman's.

The two detectives left the church as soon as the service ended around 11:30.

Even with their lunch stop at a Pizza Hut, they arrived a few minutes early at Thompson's apartment.

Caruso parked in front of Thompson's apartment building. He and Ginny waited in the car. The patrolmen and technicians arrived within the next 10 minutes. Caruso went to the building manager's apartment, showed the warrant and got the manager to unlock

Thompson's door. The manager left, and all the others entered the small apartment.

Ginny and Caruso were anxious to go through the apartment to see if they could find anything linking Thompson to Amy's murder — or to Newman's. But they restrained themselves and the patrol officers. They allowed the crime scene technicians to complete their work in each room before they entered that room. They wanted to be sure not to step anywhere or touch anything that might destroy or damage any evidence the crime scene technicians might find.

"By the way, Denny, that was pretty gutsy, telling Thompson that his tire tracks and dirt under his car matched what was at the crime scene."

"Yeah, but I felt pretty safe saying it. Thompson had admitted driving with Amy to the woods, so my lie was more of an assumption than a real lie."

"Sounds like you'll be quick enough to talk yourself into heaven when the time comes."

"Hope so. 'Cause I'm pretty sure the hard evidence will be sending me south rather than north."

Ginny couldn't help but laugh out loud.

About 20 minutes later, one of the technicians re-entered the apartment from the garage and walked up to Ginny and Caruso.

"Detectives, I think you'll owe me a nice lunch, or at least a couple of beers."

"Oh?" said Caruso.

"His car's still at his workplace, but the garage gave up a wonderful gift."

"Come on. Out with it. The suspense is killing me."

"We found a shovel. Dried dirt on it, and what looks to be dried blood. Won't know 'til the lab looks at it, but my guess is that it's dirt from the crime scene. And, I wouldn't be surprised if the blood matches that poor girl's."

"Wow!" said Ginny. "That would be a home run. Not only proof that Thompson buried her, but having the shovel with him at the crime scene is pretty strong evidence of premeditation."

"I agree," said Caruso. "But let's not get too far ahead of ourselves. Let's wait for the lab results."

"Fully agree. I'm not doing anything until we're certain. Just thinking ahead in case we get lucky."

The detectives returned to their office. Three hours later, the lab confirmed it was identical dirt and that the blood definitely belonged to Amy. In fact, they could show detailed photos of Amy's body parts to prove that the shovel was used to cut her body in pieces. They also confirmed that dirt on the bottom of a pair of work boots found in Thompson's closet matched dirt from the area where Amy's body parts had been buried. Separately, the lab confirmed that the tire tread patterns of Thompson's car matched molds they had taken at the crime scene.

Ginny and Caruso were elated. They were both upbeat when they went to bring the chief up to date. Once again, he seemed both pleased by the newly found evidence and irritated by how long it was taking to get a conviction of Amy's murderer, and to solve the Newman case.

Ginny and Caruso spent a half hour updating their paperwork and then left to start their weekends.

Chapter 33

Following his time with the Highway Interdiction Group, Joe spent two days in each of the two other units within Operations: Undercover & Surveillance and Knock & Talk. Joe found both of these to be extremely interesting, in general as well as with respect to his undercover assignment.

Undercover & Surveillance was the most glamorous and riskiest part of the task force. Undercover officers make huge personal sacrifices, sometimes rarely seeing their families for as much as two or three years. They must be on their toes 24/7; one slip-up could mean the difference between life and death for them. Most of the larger drug crime groups would not hesitate for a second before killing a discovered undercover agent working in their group. To minimize slip-ups or being unintentionally recognized, undercover agents are almost always from other parts of the state or country. They rent their own apartment and basically establish a new life for themselves. Their visits and even phone calls back to their families are kept to a minimum: In addition to not wanting to risk being seen or heard doing so, they really have to mentally and emotionally live the role they're playing, much like the best so-called method actors.

The surveillance part of this unit was more straight-forward. This group didn't have full-time members but pulled in various task force members for reasonably short assignments. Assignments were to watch known or suspected dealers and to be ready to assist whenever an undercover agent was doing something. If the criminals detected the surveillance, that surveillance assignment might be ruined, but the task force members doing the surveillance were not likely to be killed for their efforts. Joe spent two days with one of the other task force members watching the man believed to be the head of one of the largest drug dealing organizations in the area. *Hell, this is just as boring and bladder challenging as the zillion other stakeouts I've been on. Good thing it's warming up. This would be even more of a bitch if we still had full winter weather.*

Unfortunately, much of this surveillance assignment was on the weekend and Joe never made it back to Jasper Creek. Both he and Ginny were disappointed, but both were only too familiar with the fact that law enforcement is a seven-days-per-week endeavor.

Knock & talk was a totally different type of effort. Typically, two officers went to a suspect's house and, surprisingly, were usually able to get the suspect's consent for the officers to search the suspect's home. This was an effective way of obtaining evidence of a suspect's guilt. It also offered ample opportunity for a corrupt officer. The two officers typically split up to conduct the search, making it easy for one of them to stuff some drugs or cash into one of his or her pockets. By contrast, when a search was conducted with a search warrant, as many as 10 officers might be involved. With two or three officers in each room, theft was difficult unless all the officers in the room were involved.

Joe conducted three knock & talks with another officer. Drugs were found in two of the three cases, but with Joe and his partner searching different rooms, there was no way for Joe to know whether his partner was skimming drugs and/or cash.

Chapter 34

Early Monday morning, Ginny received the lab's written reports of the findings they had verbally received on Friday. Ginny called the prosecutor's office and told Atley she'd be faxing these reports to him, which Ginny did as soon as they hung up. They wanted to be sure Atley had these documents in time for the grand jury hearing.

Atley called Ginny about 10 o'clock.

"Mission accomplished."

"Wow, that was quick. Well done."

"As you know, grand juries almost always go the way the prosecutor leads them. It's clearly a one-sided process. But you guys made it even easier this time. The dirt and blood on his shovel and the dirt on his boots made this almost too easy. Thanks. And I got his arraignment hearing on the court calendar for tomorrow morning. You won't need to testify, but you might want to watch and enjoy the show."

"You bet. We'd love to."

"I'll call you tomorrow morning as soon as I have a better idea of the exact time of the hearing."

"Great. Thanks."

The next morning, Ginny and Caruso were sitting in the spectators' section when Thompson's arraignment began. It was all over 20 minutes later.

"Well, that was short and sweet," said Caruso.

"Yup. Here are the charges and here are your rights. How do you plead?"

"As expected, not guilty of course."

"Yeah," said Ginny. "The most amount of time was devoted to reaffirming Quill as his attorney, and to setting his bail."

"I was surprised it was only $150,000. Hell, he'll get that from a bondsman and be out in an hour."

"Yeah, one more example of the courts getting softer and softer on criminals. Pretty soon, they'll be releasing them before we've even had 'em processed."

"Just one of the joys of our profession."

"Denny, we're in good shape with solid evidence tying Thompson to Amy's murder. And showing it was pre-meditated. What say we go at him once more? A solid confession would be icing on the cake."

"Works for me. But let's check with the chief and with Atley before we proceed. Want to be sure we don't mess anything up at this point."

"OK. Since the idea was mine, I win. You get the chief. I'll talk with Atley."

"OK, I'll meet you back at the ranch."

Forty-five minutes later, Ginny and Caruso were back at their desks.

"Fine with the chief," said Caruso, "but he wants to view it through the one-way mirror."

"Same with Atley."

Two hours later, after a quick lunch at McDonalds, Ginny and Caruso were in the interrogation room with Thompson and his attorney. The chief and Atley were in the outer room, looking through the window and listening via the speaker.

Caruso turned on the recorder and recorded the who, where and when. "OK, let's get started."

"What's this about?" asked Quill. "You've already arrested and indicted my client. Now what?"

"We know he killed Amy Richardson. He then desecrated her body, chopping it into pieces and burying it in the woods. And we've got more than enough evidence to prove it."

"Actually, that's for the jury to decide. Not you. But, in any event, you still haven't said why we're here."

"Give us a minute. You'll soon see. And we think you'll be pleased."

"OK, I'll play. Go ahead and please me."

"Mr. Thompson," said Ginny, "as I said, we know, and have a lot of supporting evidence to show, that you killed Amy and then chopped her body into pieces and buried her in the woods. What we don't yet know is why you did it. And the why could help determine whether you're tried for first or second-degree murder. I'm sure Ms. Quill has explained to you the huge differences in penalty for these two crimes."

"But I —"

"Ethan, I told you to stay quiet. We're here to listen. I'll tell you when you can respond."

"OK."

"Anything else, Detectives?" asked Quill.

"Yes," said Ginny. "We also know that he killed Professor Newman and —"

"And what evidence might you have to support that?"

"We'll be focusing on that starting now. We don't need to spend any more time on the Richardson murder."

"And in the meantime?"

"If your client confesses to both murders and tells us why he killed them, we'll agree to second-degree murder charges, and recommend that both penalties be served simultaneously. And we'll agree to take life off the table."

"And if he doesn't agree?"

"It'll be up to the prosecutor, but our guess is that he'll go for first-degree murder, with life in prison as a real possibility."

"I'm quite sure you're bluffing, but I feel obligated to discuss all this with my client. Please give us a few minutes alone."

"Of course," said Caruso as he and Ginny left the interrogation room and the chief turned off the speaker in the room where he and Atley were watching and listening.

Fifteen minutes later, Quill knocked on the window. Ginny and Caruso walked back into the room and the chief turned the speaker back on.

"Detectives, you have a problem."

"Oh, we have a problem? Guess I was mistaken, but I thought it was your client who was indicted."

"Very funny. My client might, and I emphasize the word might, confess to the Richardson murder, but definitely not to that professor's murder. Hell, he doesn't even know who the guy is. Never heard of him until you mentioned him the other day. In this very room."

"May we ask your client a few questions?" asked Ginny.

"Sure. But we'll see whether or not I'll allow him to answer."

"Fair enough. Mr. Thompson," said Caruso, "when did you first learn about Professor Newman?"

"We already told you. The other day. When you brought him up."

"I mean, when did you first learn that he and Amy were having an affair?"

"What? You're nuts. She never slept with anyone but me."

"Ethan, please shut up," said Quill. "I'll tell you when you can speak."

"But I —"

"Ethan, shut up. Now!"

"Mr. Thompson," said Ginny, "are you trying to convince us that you never heard of the professor until the other day, that you never knew that he and Amy were sleeping together, that you never called his home phone with a burner phone and that it's just a mere coincidence that he also went missing from the same school and is dead like Amy?"

"You can believe it or not," said Quill, "but that's the truth."

"You two are good," said Caruso. "You ought to write mystery novels. Or maybe a movie."

"Very funny. So, the question for you is, purely hypothetically, what's the deal if my client pleads guilty to the girl's death and gives you all the details, but agrees to nothing about the professor? Because he didn't kill him, and you'll never be able to prove that he did."

"Fair question," said Ginny. "But we need to confer with the prosecutor before we can give you an answer. How about we call you as soon as we know something?"

"Works for us. You know where to reach me. Are we done now?"

"Most definitely. Thanks for coming in."

"Hang in there, Ethan. We should have you out on bail by dinner time."

Quill left and two officers returned Thompson to his cell. Ginny and Caruso met with Atley and the chief in the chief's office.

"Hate to say it," said the chief, "but they almost sounded believable about the professor."

"My thought exactly, Chief," said Ginny. "Walter, what can we offer them for confessing only to Richardson?"

"Let me speak with the boss. I'll get back to you sometime tomorrow."

"OK."

Atley left, but the chief motioned for Ginny and Caruso to remain.

"OK. We'll see what Atley comes back with. Either way, I think we're in pretty good shape on the Richardson case. But where the hell are we with the professor? Seems like no place to me."

"That's true, Chief," said Ginny. "But we were pretty focused on Richardson. We can now crank up our efforts on the professor."

"Well, crank away. Time's flying by and we've got nada. Other than a body, of course."

"We're on it, Chief," said Caruso with a confidence he didn't fully believe.

Caruso and Ginny headed back to their desks.

"OK. Now what?"

"Best question of the day, Ginny."

And sure enough, Thompson was released on bail in time to have dinner at home.

Chapter 35

Ginny and Caruso spent the entire next day working on Newman's murder. They reviewed their notes and re-interviewed administrators and fellow teachers at Pond View Girls Academy. Ginny scoured the internet and law enforcement databases, searching through a few additional scraps of information about Newman, while Caruso re-checked with taxi firms that might have picked him up from school or home. They again spoke with some of Amy's classmates and a few of Newman's neighbors.

"Damn. We broke our rear ends all day and have nothing to show for it."

"Well, thank you, Denny, for not showing me your broken rear end."

Despite their frustration and weariness, or perhaps because of it, both Caruso and Ginny started laughing and couldn't stop for a full two minutes.

"But you're right. We still don't have anything to go on. Hell, we don't even know where to begin. We've got his tortured body, but that's about it."

"I agree. But until something else happens or pops up, what do we do?"

"I'm afraid the answer is nothing."

"I hope you're brave enough to tell the chief that. 'Cause I'm not. He'll go off the wall before we get a chance to finish our first sentence."

"Before we speak with the chief, Denny, let's double-check Newman's laptop and cellphone. Maybe there's something there we missed."

"Works for me. Hell, in fact, anything that lets us postpone a sit-down with the chief works for me."

Just then Ginny's phone rang.

"Hello. Detective Harris."

"Hi, Ginny. This is Walter. Walter Atley."

"Hi, Walter. What did Henley decide about Thompson's plea deal?"

"That's why I'm calling. Sorry, but I haven't been able to talk with him yet. He was in court until mid-morning. Then he went right from court to a meeting with the county exec, who's apparently planning his next campaign and is locked up with all his key subordinates and staff. Latest word is that they're bringing in sandwiches and working through dinner."

"Sure, a damn political race is far more important than solving a murder case," said Ginny. "Sorry, Walter. Not mad at you. Just letting my frustration show."

"Understood. Anyhow, I should be able to grab him first thing in the morning before court starts."

"OK. And thanks for letting us know. Hopefully we'll speak in the morning."

"Yup. Good night."

"Good night."

Ginny informed Caruso, who replied, "Naturally. Why should anything go well today? That's it. Let's call it a day. The professor's laptop and cellphone will still be here tomorrow."

"Good idea. Have a good night. Starting with a stiff bourbon might help."

"Well, you finally did come up with a useful action plan. Night to you also."

Five minutes later, both detectives had pulled out of the parking lot and were on their way home.

Chapter 36

Atley called Ginny about 8:45 the next morning. "Hang on, Walter. Let me put you on speaker. Denny's here with me."

"Morning to both of you. I was able to grab Henley and he's OK with us offering second degree murder of Amy in exchange for a full confession and explanation. But he won't go with recommending a reduced sentence unless Thompson also confesses to murdering the professor. We know he committed both murders. He only gets the reduced sentence if he makes our lives easier by confessing to both the murders."

"That's still pretty good. The fact is, Thompson has no reason to confess to the second murder until we come up with some evidence. Compelling evidence, preferably."

"If you agree, I'll get Thompson's attorney over here and present the offer. I'm pretty sure she'll take it back to Thompson with a recommendation to accept it. But we'll see."

Caruso looked at Ginny, who nodded. "Works for us, Walter. Good luck. We look forward to hearing their response."

"I'll let you know as soon as I get one."

"Well, that hopefully will put the Richardson case to bed. Now let's go through the professor's laptop and cellphone," said Ginny.

"I'm with you. Let me just refill our coffee cups."

Almost three hours later, Caruso and Ginny gave up. They had found nothing useful on Newman's laptop or cellphone.

"OK, Denny. I need a lunch break. Let's go to Joe's and my favorite place."

"Wow. You going to Sancho's Taco Shop with me. Isn't that like you're cheating on Joe?"

"Yeah. Probably. But he'd understand, knowing how frustrated we both are."

"OK. So long as you mean frustrated with the Newman case."

"Yes, that's exactly what I mean. Now try to lift your mind out of the gutter."

"I'll try. But my mind is so large and amazing, it's very heavy."

Still chuckling, Ginny and Caruso headed for the door, delighted to leave their coats behind.

"Let's enjoy the walk today, Denny. Unless Mother Nature is playing one of her dirty tricks again, we may really be experiencing the end of winter."

"Sure hope so. It's already April and I'm more than ready for spring weather."

Back at their desks after a brief-but-enjoyable lunch break, Ginny saw she had a message that Atley had called her.

With Caruso at her side, Ginny called Atley and put the call on speaker.

"Hi, Walter. Sorry I missed your call. Do we have a decision?"

"Yup. Quill called. After 10 minutes of moaning and groaning about what a lousy offer we were making, she said that her client accepts the deal. Second degree on the girl, and they'll take their chances in court — if we ever get that far — on the professor's murder."

"Great. Well done. We'll get them in here today to confess with the recorder on and to write out and sign his confession. Before they change their minds."

"And I'll get to work trying to get this on the court calendar ASAP."

"Super. Speak soon."

"Bye."

Ginny and Caruso decided to take this good news to the chief right away. They thought that while he was still pleased with the confession, they could slip in the bad news about being stymied with the Newman case.

A nice-sounding strategy, but it didn't work. The chief was happy and very complimentary about the Richardson case and Thompson's confession. But his mood and tone changed very quickly when the discussion turned to the Newman case.

"Jeez. And all this time, I thought you two were detectives. Hell, I was even under the impression that the city paid you to solve crimes. How could I have been so wrong? Whaddaya mean, you've done everything possible? Twice. And now you don't even know what to do next?"

"Chief, we —"

"Don't 'Chief, we' me. Your job is to solve the damn case. Period. I don't need or want explanations why you can't. Is that understood?"

"Yes, Chief," said both detectives simultaneously.

"OK, then, get outta here. Go figure out what to do, and

then do it. If you want me to replace you on this case with a couple of competent detectives, just say the word."

"Understood, Chief. We're on it," said Caruso.

"Good. And again, well done on the Richardson case. Now do it again on this one."

Ginny and Caruso returned to their desks with their tails between their legs.

"Boy, talk about a browbeating," said Caruso.

"Yeah, but you really can't blame him. We must have looked and sounded like a couple of rookies with our fingers up our you-know-what."

"Agreed."

"I don't know how, but we better come up with something. And pretty quickly."

Despite wishing they could just go to their respective homes and climb in under the covers and hide, they forced themselves to get back to work.

An hour later, they had Thompson and Quill, along with Atley, back at the station. Thompson gave a full confession, both orally with the recorder on and in writing. He also explained what had happened.

Quill only allowed Thompson to begin his confession after Atley repeated the plea bargain offer while the recorder was on.

"This time when Amy called me for a weekend together, it was different."

"Oh, how?" asked Ginny.

"She said that she wanted to spend the weekend together with me, but it had to be different. No more kissing or sex or whatever. She just wanted us to be friends. I started arguing with her on the phone, but she cut me off pretty quick. Said she had to go meet a classmate and we could discuss it in person over the weekend."

"I guess that didn't make you too happy," said Caruso.

"Damn right. Friend. Who the hell wanted to be her friend? We were more than that, and I wasn't in the mood to step back to being her so-called friend. Can't blame me, can you?"

"I can understand that," said Caruso. "Then what happened?"

"The more I thought about it, the more pissed I got. But I figured I could fix it all when we were together that weekend."

"And?" asked Ginny.

"Fat chance. All that happened was we got into a big fight. She never admitted it, but I was sure she met someone else and was dumping me for him."

"Then?" prodded Caruso.

"The argument got more and more heated. In fact, she slapped me at one point. Pretty damn hard. I lost it. I slapped her back, squeezed her arms real hard and gave her a little push. Really, it was a soft little push. But she tripped and fell and must have hit her head or something. She looked unconscious. Or maybe even dead. Before I knew it, I got a shovel from the trunk of my car and I was hitting her with it. Pretty hard. By the time I regained my senses, she was definitely dead. Jeez, I didn't want to kill her. It musta been temporary insanity, or something like that. Know what I mean?"

"Yes, we do," said Ginny. "What did you do next?"

"Or maybe I didn't kill her with the shovel. She coulda died from the fall and hitting her head. I musta panicked.

I carried her body a few hundred feet away. Then I dug a hole. Not too deep 'cause the ground was still frozen and hard. I cut her body into smaller pieces with the shovel so it would fit into the hole, and buried her. I cleaned the shovel best I could, put it back into my car and drove home."

"Is that it?"

"Yes, I swear. The whole thing was an accident. Then I panicked and did everything else."

"Mr. Thompson," asked Ginny, "why did you initially put that shovel in your car? It's not the type of compact shovel someone would typically keep in their vehicle."

"I don't know. No reason. I guess I just did it without thinking. Maybe in case I got stuck in snow."

"Did you put it in the car because you planned to kill and then bury Amy?"

"No. No way. Or at least not consciously. Maybe it was an unconscious part of my temporary insanity."

"Yes, maybe it was."

"Mr. Thompson, what did you do with Amy's cellphone? Her pocketbook was with her body, but not her phone."

"Nothing. I have no idea. I didn't touch it. Or even see it."

Thompson nodded his head up and down as Ginny asked, "Are you sure?"

"Do you think the judge'll go easier on me 'cause of that insanity thing?"

"Don't know. We'll have to wait and see."

They all then walked over to the courthouse, where Atley had arranged for an immediate hearing on the state's request for Thompson's bail to be revoked. The hearing took only 15 minutes. Thompson's bail was revoked, and he was taken to jail to await his sentencing hearing.

Afterwards, Quill left, and Atley, Caruso and Ginny spent a few minutes bringing the chief up to date.

Back at their desks, Caruso said, "I just can't figure out what happened to Amy's cellphone. It just disappeared."

"My guess is that it fell while Thompson was killing her, and some animal grabbed it and took it back to its lair for a dinner treat. Bet he was surprised."

"You're probably right. Luckily, with the metadata from her carrier as well as being able to check Newman's phones, we didn't really need her phone."

Five minutes later, both detectives were on their way home.

Chapter 37

While Ginny and Denny were finalizing Thompson's confession and trying to make progress on the Newman case, Joe spent three days immersed in the task force's Intelligence unit. Joe found this to be among the most interesting areas of his rotation, despite it appearing to be the area least susceptible to corruption. For one thing, it was more of a virtual than real part of the task force. Although one of the task force members was supervisor of this group, the work was actually performed for the task force, and for other DEA task forces and law enforcement agencies operating in Ohio, by the Counterdrug Unit of the Ohio National Guard. These almost fifty analysts spread across the state analyzed seized drugs, linked various illegal drug organizations into networks, analyzed financial and telephone records and even provided aviation support for aerial spotting of illegal marijuana fields.

Joe drove to various parts of the state to meet with different small groups, in one case the group consisting of only two people, who worked in various Ohio National Guard facilities. Joe was surprised that such high levels of technical expertise existed anywhere within the National Guard, which up until these visits he had viewed as relatively untrained, semi-professional fighting soldiers, who were often activated by the governor to help with responses to natural disasters.

Following his visits, Joe concluded that this was probably the group least likely to be corrupt. The personnel assigned to a specific task force constantly changed, and these individuals had virtually no direct contact with the criminals or with large amounts of seized drugs or cash.

In contrast, his next rotation, three days with the Drug Diversion Group, seemed to offer significant opportunity for a corrupt task force member.

"Hi, Joe, welcome to our Drug Diversion Team. I think you'll find your few days with us very eye-opening."

"Thanks, Sergeant. I'm looking forward to it and expect to learn a lot."

"OK, then," said Sergeant George Paveglio, "let's get started. I'll give you a brief overview, then introduce you to the team and put you to work. I believe you'll really understand and appreciate what we're dealing with by actually working with our team. First off, I've been with the sheriff's office here almost twelve years now. And I've been focused on drug work almost half that time, first with the sheriff's office and, for the past three years or so, with this task force."

"And you guys focus on prescription drugs, right?"

"Correct. But it's not as simple as that may sound. Three others and I deal with this full-time. And we get a lot of help from the Intelligence Group. I know you were just with them, so I don't have to explain how they actually work through the National Guard."

"Yeah, I got that."

"They do a lot of analyses of financial reports, controlled substance tracking reports and so on for us."

"So, how big is the prescription side of the drug problem?"

"In short answer, very, very big. Opioids are prescribed almost 200 million times a year in the US. The majority of these are legitimate prescriptions for acute, or temporary, pain management. But in about 25% of the cases, the size of the prescription is for more than a 30-day supply — a real no-no with highly addictive drugs like these. More than 15% of our population has had at least one opioid prescription. About half of drug overdose deaths involve opioids, well above those involving heroin or cocaine. And the incident rate is increasing."

"Is most of this overprescribing intentional?"

"Hard to tell right now. Early on, it wasn't. Most resulted from lack of knowledge. The Center for Disease Control, the US Department of Health and a slew of local, state and professional organizations have done a pretty good job of getting the necessary info out to the doctors, nurses and hospitals. And to the public. So, today, we think that at least half the problem of overprescribing is criminal. This, of course, doesn't count all the illegal non-prescription drug importing and selling. But we're dealing with just the prescription side."

"Pretty impressive data."

"Yes, but it gets more complicated. Turns out that most who become addicted don't do so from their own over-prescription. Rather, these patients who were prescribed say a 30-day supply of opioids for a minor surgery, wind up with about an unused supply of 27 or so days. And all too often they give or sell these extra drugs to others. These others make up the bulk of those addicted to opioids and the so-called street drugs — synthetic opioids and fentanyl. These same addicts also often get their drugs by stealing them or by obtaining multiple prescriptions from multiple doctors, so-called 'doctor shopping.'"

"So who's to blame?"

"Several groups. The drug manufacturers who early on marketed their opioid products as safe and non-addictive, even though they knew or should have known otherwise. The doctors who, out of ignorance or greed, overprescribed. The drug wholesalers who knowingly shipped unbelievably large amounts of opioids to small pharmacies. These wholesalers are legally required to track and control their movement of controlled substances. Yet you hear of a pharmacy in some small town receiving enough pills in one year to supply every resident of that town with a few thousand pills. And the public, who sells or gives away the excess pills they're prescribed. And the FDA isn't blameless by any means either. In 2001, they caved to pressure from Purdue Pharmaceuticals, the manufacturer of OxyContin. Despite the lack of clinical data, the FDA, which in 1995 had approved OxyContin for use with short-term pain, expanded the label to long-term use as well. This opened the doors to tens of millions of new patients with chronic pain. Yeah, there's more than enough blame to go around."

"So where do you start?"

"That's what you're going to learn during your stay here.

First, I'm going to hook you up with Steve Goodman, who focuses on over-prescribing physicians."

"I'm ready. Let's go."

Joe's work with this section of the task force was extremely informative. Almost everything he thought he knew from newspapers and TV, as well as from the occasional drug-related case he worked on either in Jasper Creek or Chicago, turned out to be myth or, at best, more complicated than he had realized. Yes, some doctors overprescribed out of greed, but these were a relatively small proportion of the medical community. Yes, opioids often mysteriously disappeared from hospital pharmacy shelves, but this was as likely to be the result of poor or poorly enforced procedures rather than criminal intent. Yes, drug wholesalers and some pharmacies were handling far more drugs than common sense could justify, but they were doing so only in response to physicians' prescriptions.

Chapter 38

Having finished his rotation through all parts of the task force, Joe was scheduled to meet with DEA RAC Singleton on Monday in his Youngstown office. Singleton had indicated that he was anxious to hear what Joe had learned and what his suspicions might be. Then the two of them would decide how and where to place Joe in the task force for him to best be able to succeed in his undercover assignment.

For a pleasant change, Joe and Ginny agreed that Ginny would drive to Medina Friday afternoon and spend the weekend there with Joe. Joe was delighted to play host. He had made dinner reservations at two of the finer nearby restaurants and identified a number of activities for the two of them to partake in: visits to art-in-the-park, a nearby flea market, and a railway museum; hikes through the countryside; and wandering in and out of some of the quaint shops in Medina and nearby towns. They both enjoyed playing tourist for the weekend, and Ginny was pleased to see where and how Joe was living while away from home.

They also had plenty of time to talk. Joe was pleased to be able to talk through his still-forming task force conclusions with Ginny. He also wanted to hear everything about what had been going on with Ginny, understanding her need for independence but nonetheless missing the almost-nightly phone calls they used to have.

Ginny first informed Joe that the closing on her condo was scheduled for a week from Tuesday. Joe was delighted and committed to be home the weekend before to help Ginny empty out the condo. They needed to move the remainder of Ginny's clothing and personal effects, all of the furniture and decorations, and all of Ginny's files and piles of papers. Ginny had hired a cleaning service for that Monday, wanting to turn the unit over to the new owners in spic-and-span form.

Ginny also brought Joe up to date on her work-related stuff. Joe was careful to listen but not offer any suggestions or advice. All he did was nod as Ginny told him how she and Denny had learned nothing by attending both Newman's and Amy's funerals.

"Now bring me up to date on your work."

"Will do. In fact, I'm glad to have a chance to talk through it all with you. I've finished my rotation through the task force, and I have an appointment with Singleton on Monday to give him my thoughts so far. So we can decide on my next steps. And I want to tell you all about it and get your thinking and questioning of my conclusions."

"OK. I'm ready. Go for it."

"OK, let me give you a chronological summary of where I rotated when, along with my tentative conclusions about those areas most susceptible to a corrupt cop."

Joe spent the next hour or so describing the organizational units of the task force, the somewhat complicated make-up of its part-time and full-time members and what each of his rotational visits consisted of. "OK, that's about it for providing background."

"That was interesting. Now what?"

"Now I want to tell you where I think corruption is most likely and the way or ways it probably occurs. Here's where I want you to play devil's advocate, question my conclusions, make suggestions, and so on."

"Oh, goody. Now the fun begins for me," said Ginny with a big smile.

"OK. Here're where I think the system is most vulnerable, and how I think I would go about it if I were corrupt."

"Super. With all your experience, you should be more than qualified to think like a bad guy."

"Well, thank you very much — I think."

"You're most welcome."

"I see four basic areas that are the most susceptible to a dirty cop. And all of them are before the seized drugs and/or money are back in the sheriff's office. Once they're back there, the controls and accounting procedures seem to be pretty effective at keeping track of things. The first area is that of seized cash. This is easiest from highway interdictions and knock & talks. It's pretty easy for one officer, or two working together, to skim some of the cash before it's turned into the sheriff's office. This also could work with searches conducted with a search warrant, but the fact that more officers are typically doing the search in these cases complicates things. The second way is the same as number one, except they're skimming drugs rather than cash. The drugs are somewhat more difficult as they're a lot bulkier than cash."

"OK, I'm with you so far."

"Next is the skimming of cash or drugs by the under-cover buyer. All he has to do is inflate the price he had to pay. The fourth, and final, way is something akin to protection money. Get paid for warning the bad guys of an upcoming raid or undercover buy or investigation. This could be done by almost anyone in the task force with knowledge of planned efforts, from which highways will be patrolled when, to who's being surveilled or investigated. These warnings can obviously be very valuable to the bad guys."

"Joe, sounds like you've got this pretty well-covered."

"One other thing to keep in mind. It's easier to skim cash than drugs 'cause cash is much easier to hide. But skimming cash by an undercover agent conducting a buy is a bit of a problem. The task force keeping track of all the serial numbers of cash provided for a buy adds a lot of complexities to where and when to spend this cash. Skimming a dealer's cash that didn't come from the task force doesn't, of course, have these problems."

"Interesting. When you meet with Singleton, you might want to expand on which of these is easiest for one person working alone versus which more likely needs two or more bad apples to be working together."

"Good suggestion, Ginny. Thanks."

"One more thought. But this one may be a lot harder."

"Go for it."

"The question is, what's your plan to identify who's dirty and to get the evidence to prove it?"

"Yup, that is the tough part. And, at the moment, it's still a work in progress. In addition to any thoughts you have, I may need Singleton's suggestions as well."

Ginny left Sunday after an early dinner and was back home in time for a decent night's sleep.

Chapter 39

Monday evening Joe sent Ginny a text, telling her that his meeting with Singleton went well. Singleton agreed with Joe's identification of the best areas for crooked cops, and they agreed on a plan for Joe's next steps. Joe promised to fill in all the details when he came home over the weekend.

The rest of the week flew by. Ginny and Caruso spent their time completing and cleaning up their paperwork, as well as assisting two of the other detectives in talking a man down from trying to jump off the bridge over the Indian Gorge River. Joe went back to working full-time with the Highway Interdiction Unit, spending three days riding with Kenny Russo and two days with an officer he hadn't worked with before.

When Ginny got to Joe's house after work on Friday, she immediately saw Joe's car parked in the driveway. She quickly pulled in behind him and literally ran into the house, barging into Joe who, having heard Ginny pull into the driveway, was on his way to open the front door. An uncoordinated combination of hugging, kissing and laughing ensued.

"Joe, What a surprise! I didn't expect you until well after dinner."

"Yeah, well, I got permission to sneak out early. It's not every day that one of my many fiancées sells her home and officially moves in with me."

"One of your many? Have a few details you've failed to mention to me?"

"I think we have to get to know each other a little better before I start sharing all my deep, dark secrets," said Joe with a smile.

"Fair enough," said Ginny. "OK, how about I make some spaghetti and meatballs? Over our feast, you can tell me all about your meeting with Singleton and how the rest of the week went."

"Will do. Then we can make our detailed weekend to-do list for Operation Condo Sale."

"Sounds like a plan. Suggest you bulk up at dinner. You'll be working hard all weekend."

"Gotcha."

Over dinner, Joe described in detail his meeting with Singleton that past Monday.

"I've really become impressed with him. He doesn't treat you like a lowly subordinate. We had a good discussion of likeliest areas for corruption and the best way for me to proceed. We talked and challenged each other like we were two equal co-workers. And he had a lot of good thoughts and questions."

"Sounds like a good guy. So, what did you wind up concluding?"

"We agreed that I'd have a better chance of success if I'm assigned to one unit. Continuing to rotate would seem a bit weird to the others. Plus, it would make it harder, or at least take longer, to get close enough to some of the other agents and hopefully gain their confidence, and maybe even be brought into their schemes."

"I can see that."

"After agreeing on the areas with the best opportunities for a dirty agent, we decided that the Highway Interdiction Group was the best place to start. It offers one agent, or two working together, the best opportunity to be alone with seized drugs or money — or both — before any of it is counted and recorded."

"Makes sense."

"The only area that might be even better for a crooked cop is when one of the undercover agents is making a buy. But it would be hard for me to be part of the buy and able to see the actual quantities and price versus what the agent reports. Contrary to what's on TV, these undercover agents rarely wear a wire. Just too dangerous."

"So what's your plan?"

"On Monday after I got to the sheriff's office, I was permanently assigned to the Highway Interdiction Group. First, Deputy Graham called me into his office. He told me that he and Singleton decided it would be best if that was where I was assigned. When I said I was fine with that, he called in John Turner, head of that unit. John and I then went to his office, where we spent about 20 minutes going over a whole bunch of operating rules and procedures. He said he'd have me working with Kenny Russo, who he then called into his office. Had a brief intro meeting with Russo and then he and I hit the road.

"Now I need to start making some friends while keeping my eyes wide open. Should be interesting."

"Any second thoughts?"

"I often start to worry about being a rat, if you will, to fellow law enforcement officers. But then I get pissed off all over again about dirty cops and I'm good to go."

"I hear you. I think it's great what you're doing. And I'm sure you'll do a great job. Any idea how much longer it'll be?"

"No idea. Shorter rather than longer I hope. But I know I'll make a mess of it if I try to rush things. Getting close to these guys and gaining their trust will take time."

"Understood. OK, let's do the dishes and get to developing our list for tomorrow and Sunday."

"Right. By the way, dinner was super. A nice change from my normal routine of take-out or Chef Joe's fabulous cooking."

"I'll take that as a compliment. Thanks."

"You're most welcome."

Ginny and Joe finished their list, got into bed earlier than normal and spent a few minutes "getting reacquainted" with each other before they fell asleep.

They were up before seven on Saturday. The weekend flew by as they were busy making several trips by car and with a pickup truck Joe borrowed from one of his neighbors, hauling Ginny's belongings to Joe's house, Goodwill and the town dump. By Sunday afternoon, they were both exhausted and Ginny's condo was totally empty.

"Ginny, we did it. But I'm beat. I think I'll stay here tonight and then leave real early tomorrow morning to get to work on time. I'm too new to be late for work."

"Makes sense. What say we shower up and hit one of the five-star restaurants in town to celebrate? Nothing else to do tonight. Tomorrow I'll swing by the condo to check up on the cleaning service. Then Tuesday, the closing is at 10 in the lawyer's office. The chief already knows I'll be out all that morning."

"OK. Hard to imagine that by the time I see you next weekend, you'll be a lot wealthier than you are now."

"Yeah. I'll try not to spend all of it before you get back here."

Joe and Ginny had an enjoyable dinner in a nice, albeit less than a five-star, restaurant and their exhausted state helped them both have a good night's sleep.

Joe left at four the next morning and was back at the Medina County Sheriff's Office a little after seven.

Chapter 40

Ginny was up bright and early Tuesday morning. She thought she had become totally comfortable with selling her condo, but, much to her surprise, the thought of the closing kept her awake a good part of the night and woke her early. She was less comfortable with the sale than she thought she'd be. She wasn't sure if it was simply nostalgia for a place she'd owned and lived in for so many years or if it was more a loss of freedom and reaching the point of no return in her relationship with Joe. She was sure she loved Joe, deeply, but marriage was a big and, hopefully, irreversible move. She was sure she'd get over these feelings, but, at that moment, they left an empty hole in the pit of her stomach. *What if I don't ever get over these feelings? I can't even tell Joe about them — he'd never understand and would wind up mad or hurt or, most likely, both.* Ginny continued struggling with these thoughts as she showered, dressed and had breakfast. *What the hell is wrong with me? Everything is finally going close to perfectly for me. I couldn't ask for anyone better than Joe. And yet here I am feeling sorry for myself.*

By the time she had to leave, Ginny had pulled herself together. She was at the lawyer's office by 9:30, and by 11:15 she had swapped her condo for a large certified check. She swung by the bank and deposited the check into a newly opened money market account and headed to work. *OK, now we start the next chapter in the life of Virginia Harris.*

When Ginny got to her desk, she sent a short text to Joe: "Condo sold. Money in the bank. Onwards & upwards. Love." Less than a minute later, she received Joe's response: "Congrats! Glad you haven't spent it all on shoes. Love back atcha."

Chapter 41

Three weeks later, the day for Thompson's sentencing hearing arrived.

Ginny and Caruso walked over to the courthouse.

"Finally! Spring has fully and definitely reached Ohio."

"Fantastic, Denny. What a pleasure to just wear a light sweater instead of a heavy coat."

"Not to mention hat and gloves. And, all too often, boots. When I eventually retire, you and Joe are welcome to come visit me in Florida."

"Deal. And you can be sure that all of our visits will be during the winter."

Ginny and Caruso entered the courthouse and grabbed two seats, about two-thirds of the way back in the packed spectators' area.

The judge had Thompson stand and admit he killed, desecrated the body of and then buried Amy. He allowed Thompson to state that he thought he might have suffered from temporary insanity, but he cut Thompson off whenever he started into a detailed description of his insanity and not knowing why he did what he did.

The judge then had Quill and Atley review the terms of the plea deal and confirm that both parties were in agreement with it.

After offering the chance for anyone who wished to speak on behalf of the defendant or the victim to do so, an offer which no one accepted, the judge was ready to impose the sentence.

"Will the defendant please stand." It grammatically sounded like a question, but the judge's tone made clear that it wasn't. Quill and Thompson stood.

"Mr. Thompson, the court accepts your plea of guilty to the murder of one Amy Richardson. I am hereby sentencing you to the sentence to which you and the prosecutor's office have agreed. For the crime of second-degree murder of Amy Richardson, I hereby sentence you to life imprisonment in the state prison at the Chillicothe Correctional Institution in Chillicothe, Ohio. You will be escorted to said facility immediately upon completion of this hearing. You will be eligible for parole after serving 20 years. Is that clear?"

"Yes, your honor," mumbled Thompson.

The sheriff's deputies cuffed Thompson and led him out of the courtroom.

Mr. and Mrs. Richardson, who had been in the first row of spectators, walked over to Ginny, Caruso and Atley.

"Thank you for this," said Mrs. Richardson. "It, of course, won't bring our Amy back to us, but it's comforting to see her killer getting the punishment he deserves."

"Damn right," said her husband. "Although I would have preferred to spend 10 minutes alone with him while I had a shovel in my hands. That would have been real justice."

"We understand. But I'm sure you know that would not have been the right way to do it."

"Yeah, I guess so. Can I ask you a question?"

"Of course," answered Caruso.

"How sure are you that he was the killer? Is there any chance that it was someone else? Or that someone did it with him?"

"Mr. Richardson, let me assure you," said Ginny. "We are as certain as we can be, given our investigation, the evidence we found and his confession, that Mr. Thompson did it. And we've seen nothing to suggest that he didn't act totally alone. Why do you ask? Do you have any reason to doubt this? Are you aware of something we're not?"

"No! Not at all. Just want to be sure."

"Well, I think you can be sure in this case."

"OK, thanks."

"Yes, thank you all again," said Mrs. Richardson.

After the Richardsons left, Ginny, Caruso and Atley spent a few minutes congratulating each other and enjoying the successful conclusion of this case. They then left the by-then almost empty courtroom.

Back at their desks, Ginny and Caruso enjoyed the congratulations from the other detectives in the room. But that didn't last long. They were soon once again lamenting their total lack of progress, and lack of even an action plan, on the Newman murder.

"Damn," said Ginny. "It's been two months and we've got shit. A tortured body we don't seem able to make anything of. No leads, no plan. I think we gotta talk with the chief. Again. Either he's got some suggestions for us, or he ought to give this to another team. Or, maybe it's time to unofficially consider it a cold case."

"Yeah. And just hope and wait that something develops someday. Boy, what a crappy feeling."

"Tell me about it."

The chief clearly was as unhappy about this case as he had been before, but he agreed to leave it with Ginny and Caruso.

"OK, it's still your case. I understand you won't be spending much, or perhaps even any, time on it until you think of something new and different or something pops up. So, it's sort of a cold case, but I don't want us to officially classify it that way. At least not yet. It's still too hot a topic. If anyone asks, 'we continue to pursue all leads and have nothing to report at this time.' In the meantime, go solve some of the other cases on your desk."

"Will do," said Ginny as she and Caruso returned to their desks and their other open cases.

Chapter 42

Two weeks later, around three in the afternoon, the chief summoned Ginny and Caruso to his office.

"Uh oh," said Ginny. "Time for another reaming, given our lack of progress on the Newman case."

"Yup," said Caruso. "Hate to say it, but you can't really blame him. Hell, we're still no place with the damn case. Labeled a cold case or not, it's pretty damn ice cold."

"Sit down," said the chief as Ginny and Caruso entered his office.

"Chief," said Ginny, "we know what you're going to say and we —"

"How about you just be quiet for a minute and let me say what *I* know I'm going to say?"

"Sure, Chief, just trying to let you know we understand."

"Whatever you think this is about, I'm sure you're wrong. Need you two to head over to Memorial."

"Oh," said Ginny. "We thought this was going to be about the Newman case."

"That's the question."

"Huh?" said Caruso.

"Turns out the medics just brought Mr. Richardson, Amy's father, into the ER. Apparent attempted suicide."

"Jeez," said Caruso.

"Man, he took Amy's death worse than we imagined."

"Seems so. But I want you two to talk with him. He's

awake, but they're going to hold him overnight for observation."

"What a shame. Haven't he and his wife been through enough? OK, we're on our way now."

Ginny led Caruso out of the chief's office and down to her car.

Fifteen minutes later, they were talking with the nurse sitting at the third-floor nurses' station.

"So, what can you tell us?"

"Not much to tell. The medics brought him in about two hours ago. Several cuts on his left wrist, but clearly an amateurish attempt. No way he's going to kill himself the way he was cutting. In fact, he's here more for psych than physical reasons."

"Has he said why he was trying to commit suicide?"

"No. He hasn't said anything of substance."

"Who called 9-1-1?" asked Ginny.

"His wife. She said she got home from the supermarket and found him in the bathroom cutting his wrist."

"Is Mrs. Richardson here?" asked Ginny.

"Yes, she's in his room with him."

"Oh. OK. We're going to talk with them now." As the nurse started to get up, Ginny continued, "No need to escort us. They know both of us."

"OK, then." Pointing to her left, she continued, "It's 344, fourth room on the right."

"Thanks."

Ginny and Caruso stood in the doorway as Ginny knocked on the open door.

Mrs. Richardson looked up, immediately recognized the detectives and waved them in.

"Mrs. Richardson, hello," said Ginny. "Mr. Richardson, how are you feeling?"

Mrs. Richardson said hello, while her husband remained silent and turned away.

"Mrs. Richardson, let's you and I go outside and talk for a few minutes," said Ginny.

Mrs. Richardson got up and she and Ginny left the room, walked down the hall and found an empty small waiting room where they sat down to talk. Caruso remained in the room with Mr. Richardson.

Ginny learned little from Mrs. Richardson that she didn't already know. Mrs. Richardson did say that her husband seemed to take Amy's death very hard and seemed unable to start getting over it. In fact, he seemed to be getting increasingly more depressed as time went on. She even had to call his employer about a week ago and arrange for a leave of absence for him.

Caruso was more successful with Mr. Richardson.

"It was my fault. How could I have been so stupid? And impulsive. What an idiot!"

"Mr. Richardson, don't blame yourself. There was nothing you could have done to prevent your daughter's murder. Believe me."

"I know."

"Excuse me?"

"I'm talking about him."

"Him? Mr. Thompson? What about him?"

"No. Not him. I mean that teacher."

"Professor Newman? The chemistry teacher from Amy's school who was killed?"

"Yes. Him."

"What about him? Do you know what happened to him?"

"Yes. Isn't that why you're here?"

"Mr. Richardson, please tell me whatever you know about Professor Newman."

With tears welling up in his eyes and his cheeks turning red, Mr. Richardson said, "I killed him."

"You killed him? Why? How? Please. Tell me everything."

"I was an idiot. I was sure he was responsible for Amy going missing. I knew that Amy sometimes went back to his classroom for tutoring in the late afternoon last year when she was in his chemistry class. And that continued this year even though she wasn't in any of his classes. She was also always going on about what a great teacher and wonderful, caring person he was. I became convinced that they were, uh, involved with each other. You hear and read so much about teachers getting sexually involved with their students. Pretty damn sick. And Amy didn't seem to have much interest in boys her own age, so I figured out why. Or at least I thought I did."

"Did you talk to anyone, your wife or someone at the school, about your beliefs?"

"No. I didn't want to get my wife upset."

"So then what happened?"

"After Amy was missing for about a week, and no one, including the police, had any idea what had happened or where she was, I decided I better act before it was too late. I was sure Amy had run off and that she and the professor were secretly meeting."

"So what did you do?"

"I called the professor and explained that I needed his help. That I had some ideas about Amy's whereabouts, but I needed to check a few details with him. He agreed to see me that Sunday morning. I arranged to pick him up around the corner from his house at eight."

"Did you call him at home or at the school? Or on his cellphone?"

"His home number. That was the only one I could find in the phone book."

"And where did you call him from?"

"I bought a prepaid cellphone to call him. And then I crushed and threw the phone away."

"Where'd you buy the phone?"

"Not sure of the name. It was one of those discount electronic stores. In the sleazy part of Dayton."

"What happened next?"

"We met as agreed and I told him I had to take him to see something. He was a little uncomfortable, but he said OK."

"Where'd you take him?"

"I drove to Overlook Pass. After I parked at one of the scenic stopping areas, I accused him of having an affair with Amy, of encouraging her to run off and, of course, of knowing where she was. I demanded that he tell me everything. He denied everything. The louder my accusations, the louder and firmer his denials. I started slapping and punching him. He was pretty thin and weak and couldn't really fight back much. The more he denied things, the more I hit him. I was really getting frustrated. And pissed."

"What happened next?"

"He tried to get out of the car, but I think my beating him prevented it. Heck, he couldn't even unbuckle his seat belt. I mean, he was like punch-drunk."

"And then?"

"I pretty well lost it. I beat him up badly, but he kept saying he was not involved with Amy and didn't know where she was. Then I actually started torturing him. I burned him with my cigarette and even cut him with my pocketknife. Hell, I even think I might have broken some of his fingers. My God, I can't believe what I did."

"Then what happened?"

"I dragged him out of the car. Kept punching and kicking him. He barely put up any resistance. His body finally went limp. I half-carried, half-dragged him to the edge. I told him I'd push him over if he didn't tell me where Amy was."

"And then?"

"I started shaking him, more and more violently as he refused to tell me. Then, he slipped out of my hands. I stood there and watched him bounce from rock to rock as he fell all the way down."

"Then what did you do?"

"His body was very visible from where I was standing. I knew I had to hide him. Luckily, the road back down from Overlook Pass goes almost next to where his body was lying. I drove down there. It wasn't easy, but I got him into my trunk. Then I drove and dumped the body where I thought it wouldn't be easily found."

"Where was that?"

"I drove out to Crystal Lake and hid him in the grass and weeds under some bushes next to the water. I figured his body would decay before he was found."

"Then what?"

"I drove home. I wiped down the inside of the car and the trunk. And the passenger door to get rid of any of his fingerprints. I burned my clothing out back and then took a shower. I didn't feel guilty about killing him, just upset that he died before telling me where Amy was. And now it turns out she was murdered by that Thompson boy. Damn, the teacher's denials were true all along. What the hell was wrong with me?"

"Mr. Richardson, you were a distraught father. Trying to find and save his daughter. But now, I need you to repeat what you told me while I record it, and then I also need you to put it in writing. Let me read you your Miranda rights first, just to make it all kosher."

"Sure. Whatever you want. I deserve whatever happens to me. I killed a totally innocent man."

Caruso called Ginny on her cellphone and filled her in. Ginny had Mrs. Richardson go down to the cafeteria for a cup of coffee, promising to get her when they were ready. She then checked with the physician treating Mr. Richardson. He confirmed that Mr. Richardson was on a mild tranquilizer, but nothing that would alter his mental abilities. Ginny then returned to Richardson's room.

After being read his Miranda rights, Richardson repeated his story while being recorded. He also wrote it out longhand.

Ginny went down to the almost-empty cafeteria and filled Mrs. Richardson in on the latest developments.

What a disaster. First her only child, and now her husband. Caruso stayed with Mr. Richardson until the patrol officer he requested arrived. The police would stay in his room to prevent any possible escape or additional suicide attempts until he was released from the hospital the next day.

Ginny and Caruso were back at their desks just before eight that evening. Using a speaker phone, they called the chief at home and brought him up to date. Turned out to be one of the few times he was complimentary without adding any "but" before the conversation ended. Ginny also called Atley, but got his voicemail. She left a brief summary of all that had happened and asked that he call her in the morning.

Ginny and Caruso spent a few minutes reflecting how, after being totally stymied week after week on this case, the solution just fell into their laps. Relieved and pleased, but feeling bad for both Mr. and Mrs. Richardson, they said good night to each other and headed home.

Chapter 43

*L*ate the next morning, Mr. Richardson was released by the hospital and immediately arrested by the police.

While he was locked in one of the interrogation rooms at the police department, Ginny and Caruso were discussing their next steps.

Ginny had spoken with Atley and brought him up to date. He agreed to be at the station right after lunch, at 12:30 or so.

"Denny, I'm happy to run out and grab us a couple of lunches."

"Great. I'm starved."

"Let me just check. Might as well bring something back for Richardson as well."

"Yeah. This may be his last gourmet meal for a while."

"I agree. Assuming you view Burger King as a gourmet kind of place."

"I've eaten a lot worse."

Ginny checked with Richardson, walked the three blocks to Burger King and was soon back with burgers, fries and Diet Cokes for the three of them. Richardson ate alone in the interrogation room, while Ginny and Caruso ate at their desks, with Caruso using Joe's desk directly across from Ginny's.

"Richardson did indicate he'd like his lawyer present. He gave me his name and number. Called him while I was waiting at Burger King for our lunch order. Our good friend, David Coleman. He'll be here as close to 12:30 as he can."

"Good old Coleman. Haven't seen him in, probably, a year or so. He usually manages to represent the worst of the worst, but it's mostly white-collar crime kinda stuff, not murder."

"I guess he's the only defense attorney Richardson has ever needed or dealt with until now."

"Most likely. Be interesting to see if Coleman sticks with this until the end, or recommends a more suitable attorney, one experienced with serious stuff like murder."

"We'll see," said Ginny with a shrug.

"With his signed confession, this should be pretty short and sweet."

"I would think so. But I really feel for him. I can't begin to imagine having your only child disappear and you're confronting the person you're sure was the cause of the disappearance."

"I understand. But he did murder Newman. Even if he says he didn't mean to. But then not calling 9-1-1 doesn't exactly help his case."

"I know. I know. But still…"

Shortly after 12:30, while Ginny and Caruso were at their desks waiting for Atley, Coleman arrived. After saying hellos to each other, Caruso gave Coleman a quick summary of the situation and then led him to the interrogation room. Caruso left Coleman with his client.

"Hi, David. Thanks for coming so quickly."

"Don't mention it. What the hell happened? You're being charged with murder."

"Well, I should be. I murdered him."

"And I understand you already confessed. Usually better to meet with your lawyer before rather than after you confess."

"Yeah, I know. It all just seemed to happen so fast."

"OK. Let's go back to the beginning. Tell me the whole story."

And that's what Richardson did. Starting with his daughter's disappearance all the way up to his arrest earlier in the day.

"Wow. That's quite the story. First off, my most sincere sympathies about your daughter. But right now we have to focus on you. As you know, I'm not an expert in murder defense work by any means. So any time you become uncomfortable with me representing you, just say so and I'll help get you someone else. There'll be no hard feelings. And if I, at any time, begin to feel out of my league, I'll find someone else to represent you. OK?"

"OK."

After Atley arrived, Ginny knocked and walked into the interrogation room. She said they'd be in shortly, that Atley had just arrived and she and Caruso wanted to bring him up to speed before they all got started.

At a little after one, they were all in the interrogation room.

Caruso indicated he'd be recording the session, and began by stating the when, where and who of the session. He also stated, and had Richardson confirm, that Richardson had confessed on tape and in writing after having been read his Miranda rights.

"I'd like a copy of that written confession," said

Coleman. "I'd also like to know exactly what charges you plan to file."

"The detectives and I discussed that a few minutes ago. We are sympathetic to Mr. Richardson being distraught about his daughter and thinking, even though he was wrong, that Professor Newman was behind it all. Nonetheless, he did commit murder."

"And, therefore?" prompted Coleman.

"If your client pleads guilty, we're willing to go with voluntary manslaughter, with, as you know, a three to 11-year sentence. But, if not, we'll be looking at second degree, probably with an obstruction charge thrown in. Mr. Richardson, just so you know, the second-degree murder charge, without the obstruction charge, carries a 15-year to life sentence."

"Is that the best you can do?"

"Yes, it is, David. And I don't know how long I can leave this offer sitting out there."

"May I have a few minutes with my client, please? And please bring me a copy of his written confession."

"Sure," said Ginny as she, Caruso and Atley stood up and left the room.

"What does all that mean?" asked Richardson.

"Simple. If you stick with your confession and plead guilty, you'll most likely get five to eight years in prison. If we plead not guilty and lose, you're probably looking at thirty years with no parole possibilities before year 20."

"Well, I did do it, so I should plead guilty. Even though it was an accident."

"Hold on. Let's not rush into anything. I want to read your confession first. Then I'd like to consult with some experts. We might have a shot at a temporary insanity plea. Or perhaps something else. You hiding the body makes accidental a tough argument. We don't have to decide anything until after the grand jury hearing."

"OK. You're the boss."

Coleman signaled for the others to come back in. He then informed them that he and his client needed a few days to sort everything out. He committed to respond to the guilty plea offer within a couple of days, Monday at the latest.

Caruso then took Richardson for processing and booking. Ginny gave Coleman a copy of the confession. The attorneys left and Ginny gave the chief an update on the meeting. The chief again seemed satisfied and managed not to make any derogatory comments. *Wow, the chief is now two-for-two. He must have changed his breakfast cereal. Or something. I just wonder how long this can last.*

Ginny filled Caruso in when he returned from booking Richardson. Soon after, Caruso and Ginny were both gone for the night.

Chapter 44

Two months later, Ginny and Caruso watched the final steps of their case play out. Having already had the grand jury hearing, the indictment of Mr. Richardson and his guilty plea, the short, almost perfunctory, sentencing hearing was held. After the judge led the defense and prosecutor through the pre-arranged song and dance, Mr. Richardson was sentenced to a 10-year term, with eligibility for parole after six years. The judge sentenced him to serve his time at the Southeastern Correctional Complex in Lancaster, slightly less than a two-hour drive from Jasper Creek.

"At least he won't be too far away for his wife to visit," said Ginny.

"Yeah, and if they're lucky, he's paroled after six years."

"I sure hope they can get their lives back together again. They, especially him, weren't exactly parents of the year, but no one deserves what they're going through."

"In a way, what happened to them could happen to any one of us."

"Agreed. I don't know, Denny. Hard to tell if he's more of a victim or a criminal."

"That's 'cause he's both. Father of a murdered daughter and, despite his thinking that he had good reason, murderer of an innocent man."

"Suppose so. Well, we did our jobs. And the end result is what it is."

"Yup."

"OK. Let's head back. We can fill the chief in on the sentencing, and then see what he's got for us next."

Chapter 45

Over the weekend about three weeks later, Ginny and Joe discussed the successful conclusion of Newman's murder investigation.

"Again, Ginny, I tip my hat to you and Denny for sticking with this and finally solving it."

"Thanks, Joe. The good news is that, contrary to our worst fears, turns out we weren't dealing with a serial killer after all. And I appreciate how I'm sure you often bit your tongue to avoid giving me too much advice. I'm sure it wasn't easy for you, but it did help me rebuild some of my lost confidence."

"Glad to hear it. But I wasn't really biting my tongue, I just had no new ideas."

"Whatever. I still can't get over Mr. Richardson. From a largely absent, non-caring parent, he suddenly starts caring so much about his missing daughter that he kills Newman. I don't get it."

"That's why Dr. Freud asked me to explain things to you."

"Oh, good. Please do tell, Sigmund, Junior."

"I do think that he cared about Amy. It's just that he cared about himself and his wife more. He was happy when Amy didn't interfere with their lives. Probably why she roomed at school despite living nearby. A credit card with ATM access so she could pay for whatever she needed or wanted without bothering her parents. Given all of her prior absences, her parents were pissed at her running away again. Based on the prior episodes, they had no reason at first to be worried about her. They only started to worry as the length of her absence grew."

"I'm with you so far."

"Then as her absence continued, guilt popped its ugly head in the door. Guilt at initially blaming Amy for another runaway. Guilt at continuing to focus on his work and leaving everything, including that press conference, on his wife's shoulders. I think the guilt drove him to need to somehow take control and actively try to find and save his daughter. Based on all the publicity of teachers getting involved with students, how much Amy used to rave about Newman, how he knew that Newman used to tutor Amy privately when she was in his class and even this year when she wasn't, and who knows what else, he convinced himself that Amy and Newman had arranged for Amy to run off and then hook up someplace with Newman. Hell, he might even have somehow learned about Newman's recent divorce, thereby adding more fuel to the fire."

"That makes sense, Joe."

"Yeah, maybe. Or probably. We, and even good old Sigmund, have to be very careful about ever thinking we fully understand why somebody does something. But this probably isn't too far from the truth."

"Agreed. And thanks. Now let me bring you up to date about the Denny and Ginny duo. The chief officially decided to have Denny and me remain partners until you return."

"That's good. As we've said, he's one of the good ones, and you and he seem to work well as partners."

"Yup. He's my second-best partner."

"Oh? And who might be number one?"

"I'd tell you, but I wouldn't want your head to swell too much."

"Gotcha. So, what have you and your second-best partner been keeping busy with, now that you solved the Amy and Newman murders?"

"Just doing an amazing job of helping to clean up several members of the Jasper Creek criminal element. Thanks to video cameras, we identified and arrested two bums who were robbing convenience stores all over town. Once they and their lawyers saw the videos, they both copped quick confessions, both racing to claim the other one was the mastermind of the crime wave."

"Good for you guys."

"And that's not all. We're not just one-trick ponies. We arrested another fine citizen who had a pleasant hobby of beating his wife most every night. Typical unfortunate situation where she was afraid to leave or call the authorities. Happily, there were no kids involved. This last time, he actually broke her jaw and she wound up in the ER. They admitted her to the hospital, and we had a few days to talk with her while her husband was prevented from seeing or talking with her. We convinced her to file a complaint, after which we happily arrested the son of a bitch. For a bit there, I didn't think I'd be able to calm Denny down and prevent him from beating the shit out of the guy. I was really worried for a few minutes, but Denny came to his senses. Thank goodness."

"Amen to that. A beating sure wouldn't have helped the prosecution. Or Denny's career either. Sounds like you two have been busy."

"Yes, we have. We just happened to luck out with a couple of cases that broke for us pretty quickly."

"That's good. Partially makes up for the drawn-out problems with the student's and professor's killings."

"True. And I also have to say, it helped with my self-confidence that I didn't have to keep running to you for help and advice."

"Ginny, I —"

"No need to say anything, Joe. I meant that as a positive thing."

Chapter 46

For about two more months after Richardson's sentencing, Joe continued working with Russo in the Highway Interdiction unit. Although they never discussed or agreed to it, they alternated days as driver or passenger. The dark blue, two-year-old Ford Bronco was pleasant to drive and powerful enough to easily keep up with and pass the other vehicles on the highway.

They spent most of each day driving back and forth on 100-plus miles of highway, averaging about two vehicle stops per day. Joe was never able to fully relax, despite the often low-stress time just traveling the highway. *I feel like a liar. Here we are getting to know each other, even sharing somewhat personal information. And all the while, I'm sitting here trying to figure out how to best catch Kenny stealing drugs or money. I know I'm doing this for a good cause, but still...* Joe only became more upset with his role as he learned about Russo's wife, their 18-month-old baby boy and child number two expected in four months. *Damn, do I really want to catch this guy stealing? Well, I guess the whole answer is that I hope he's not stealing, but if he is, yes, I do want to catch him.*

On some of their vehicle stops, they were joined by another pair of task force members. But on several, they weren't. It was on these stops when they weren't joined by others that Russo would have the best chance to steal as he and Joe split up, one searching the vehicle they stopped and the other staying with the vehicle driver and any passengers. When they found drugs, it was usually Russo who drove the suspected criminals, the drugs (if compact enough to fit in the Ford Bronco), and money (if any) back to the sheriff's office while Joe waited with the vehicle for a tow truck. Russo's time alone offered him the safest opportunity to skim some drugs or money.

Joe realized that it would be a long time before Russo or anyone else felt close enough to Joe to confide in him about any corrupt activities and perhaps invite him to join in. Joe also realized that it was almost impossible to determine whether Russo was skimming when Russo was all alone with the drugs or money. Joe arranged an evening meeting with Singleton at a rest stop halfway between their two locations.

"Good evening, Joe. What a surprise to bump into you here."

"Yes, sir. Quite a coincidence, indeed."

"What's up? You made it sound pretty important when you called."

"Yes, it is." After describing his inability to view Russo or any other task force member skimming, Joe said, "But I have an idea — if we can arrange it."

"OK. What's your idea?"

"If we, that is you, can arrange it, a few fake drug runs would be ideal. In addition to recording the serial numbers of money they're transporting, we could add a harmless but identifiable chemical to the drugs on board. It would then be relatively easy for us to track both the money and the drugs, and use that to lead us to the dirty agents."

"Hmm. Interesting idea. I'm sure I can arrange the fake drug runs, but how do we handle the drivers and any passengers? I don't think putting a few of our guys in prison for a few years would be well-received."

"I'm sure not. Could you get the drivers and passengers from other DEA undercover activities elsewhere in the country? Give them fake identities. Then after they're arrested here, have some of them extradited to other parts of the country for alleged prior federal charges or something. Others could be let out on bail and then disappear into the wind. They, with their fake identities, all just fall off the grid and go back to their regular jobs."

"Hey, you've really thought this through, Joe. It'll take some doing and coordination, but I'm pretty sure we could make it work."

"The advantage is that, with the serial numbers known for any money and a different chemical added for each fake vehicle run or drug bust, we can check on a bunch of officers simultaneously. I wouldn't have to be with them or even know them for this to work. And to totally package the proof, we'd need to know the schedule of what each officer was assigned to over what time period."

"Very ingenious. I like your thinking. Give me a couple of days to work the details out with a few of my DEA buddies elsewhere in the country, and we should be good to go."

"Sounds good to me."

"OK, Joe. Thanks. I'll be in touch when we're ready to move. Why don't you think about who you'd most trust to keep providing us with work schedules so we know which agent is doing what?"

"Will do."

Joe and Singleton said their good-byes and each headed home.

Joe was up early the next morning. Over breakfast, he thought through whom he most trusted to give him the work schedules. *Damn, if I pick the wrong person, this whole investigation, and me with it, is blown. Regardless, I have to pick someone. To me, there's only one person I feel good trusting — Gretchen Werner, Graham's administrative assistant. She was extremely helpful to me and I feel like we established some kind of relationship when she helped me find an apartment. She's worked here forever and seems to know everyone and everything going on. The key will be if she's comfortable with not even telling her boss about this. Graham seems like a good guy and is most likely honest, but you can never be sure. Even Singleton didn't want to share my assignment with him, so I definitely shouldn't. I think I'll invite Werner out for lunch tomorrow, then feel her out while we're off campus.*

Chapter 47

Joe's lunch with Werner was a success. She was initially surprised when Joe told her of his undercover assignment, but she quickly adjusted to it, admitted recognizing the need for it and agreed to help. She was concerned about doing this behind Graham's back, but she agreed to do it. She felt that if her role in this ever became known, Graham would accept and forgive her once he learned that Singleton demanded she keep this secret from everyone. Werner understood the importance of — and agreed to — never divulging Joe's involvement in trying to bring down the corrupt agents.

Singleton was effective in coordinating the setups with two of his long-term DEA buddies, both now resident agents in charge, one outside Vancouver, Washington, and the other in Houston.

Over a four-month period, seven staged vehicle runs were conducted. Prior to each of the runs, the task force was alerted to the suspected run with a vehicle description, date and approximate time provided. Six of the seven vehicles were stopped by task force members working highway interdiction. Two of these six stops were made by Joe and Russo. These six stops showed three of the agents to be skimming. *Damn, I wish Kenny hadn't been one of them. What the hell was he thinking? Especially with one young child and another on the way.*

Or maybe it was, in fact, the kids and the future expenses that drove him to do this. The two others were a pair of agents who were partners. Joe had met them but didn't know them well.

As planned, in each case, those in the vehicle carrying drugs were arrested, and soon "extradited" to other parts of the country or released on bail. Four other corrupt agents were also identified: two doing searches following knock & talks and two associated with undercover drug buys. The corrupt agents weren't initially charged with anything; Singleton and Joe wanted to wait until their operation was complete before alerting anyone to the fact that an undercover investigation was underway.

The day Joe learned that Russo was one of the dirty task force members was Joe's worst day on the task force. He spent most of the night tossing and turning. He had a total of three or so hours of sleep, made up of what felt like a series of 20-minute naps. At one point he was wide awake, staring into the mirror above the bathroom sink.

Dammit, why'd Russo have to be one of the dirty ones? He and I were starting to become friends. No way did I even think he might be dirty. Shit, I must be losing my touch. No matter, he and the other ones gotta get convicted. They made their own beds and now they have to sleep in them.

The worst possible outcome would be that they get indicted but wind up not getting convicted. The evidence is pretty good, but you can never tell when a jury gets involved. I can't believe I'm thinking what I'm thinking. But I've learned enough on this assignment to see how I can snatch some evidence from a few knock & talks. Damn easy to plant some of it on each of the dirty ones to ensure their conviction. Not like I'd be sending anyone innocent to prison. Just making sure Lady Justice doesn't screw up.

Slamming his fist against the wall next to the mirror, Joe continued thinking, *Jeez, I'm as bad as they are. Decided to be a rat 'cause of how much I hate dirty cops and now here I am planning out the details of how I can become a dirty cop. What the hell is wrong with me? I've never planted or even seriously considered planting evidence. Not in Chicago, and not in Jasper Creek. Hell, if I do this now, it'll probably become a regular thing for me going forward.* Realizing that he had been tightly gripping the sink to prevent his hands and arms from shaking, Joe deliberately relaxed his grip. *No way! I don't want to be that kind of cop. My whole career, I've hated when others planted evidence. And I sure as hell don't want Ginny to see me as one of those dirty cops.*

Joe stripped off his shorts and jumped into the shower. He hadn't realized how sweaty he'd become. He climbed back into bed and fell back asleep after a half hour or so of tossing and turning.

Chapter 48

Joe and Singleton met to be sure they were set to shut their operation down.

"Well done, Joe. Thanks to you, we're ready to charge our seven bad apples. And we've got the evidence to be pretty sure they'll all be convicted."

"Thanks. But I wish there had been a lot fewer dirty agents. Hell, this is a big hunk of the whole task force."

"I agree. But the good thing is we caught them. And we learned a few things."

"Like what?"

"For one thing, don't keep anyone on the task force for more than, say, three years. And during that three years, change their assignments and partners often enough that they can't build up routines or develop confederates."

"Good points. So, what're your next steps?"

"Next week we're going to indict all seven of them. Although it'll take several months for all the trials, they'll be suspended or at least assigned desk duty in the interim. And this should serve as a nice warning to everyone else now on the task force and those who join in the future. Also to those on other task forces."

"Glad I was able to help."

"We couldn't have done it without you, Joe. And the good news is that, so far, best we can tell, no one has any idea of your involvement in all this."

"That's good."

"I suggest you remain on the task force for a couple more months and then head back to your regular job in Jasper Creek. It would raise a lot of suspicions if you left right after all the indictments. Plus, with all these indictments, we can use you on the task force until we get it re-staffed."

"Works for me."

And that's exactly what happened. The seven were indicted, over the next eight weeks or so most of them were replaced on the task force and shortly thereafter, Joe left the task force for so-called "personal reasons" and returned to the Jasper Creek PD.

Over the next 15 months, all seven of those charged were convicted, including three who pleaded guilty. Five were given prison sentences and two were released with heavy community service obligations. All saw an abrupt end to their law enforcement careers.

Chapter 49

*I*n early April, thirteen months after the chief first mentioned the task force, Joe was back at Jasper Creek PD. He and Ginny were sitting in the chief's office, with his door closed.

"Welcome back, Joe. And job well done. I spoke with Singleton and he's very pleased with your work and the results that were accomplished."

"Thanks, Chief. And thanks for the opportunity, despite my initial bitching about task forces."

"No problem. And, by the way, Singleton asked me to tell you that if you ever have any interest in going to work for the DEA, he'd be happy to provide the right introductions and recommendations."

"Nice. But, at least for now, I'm happy to be back here."

"Works for me. Let's go out and announce your official return and inform Denny that he'll need to trade in his partner for someone else."

Joe was pleasantly surprised at the natural and friendly welcome he received from all his coworkers. Within 10 minutes, he almost felt as if he had never left the department.

"Thank you. Thank you, all. I must admit, despite the interesting and, I think, useful stint on the drug task force, it's good to be back home. Some of you, in fact, probably all of you, have heard me complain about some of the task forces I was on back in Chicago. I expected the same BS and bureaucracy this time. But I was pleasantly surprised. There was a minimum of that, and most of the task force members, including the suits, are good folks dedicated to doing the job and getting some of the huge amounts of drugs, and the criminals behind them, off the street. If any of you ever get the opportunity like I did, I strongly recommend you grab it. I don't think you'll be disappointed."

Joe then put up with about 10 minutes of good-natured ribbing.

"OK, enough of this mushy stuff," said Ginny. "You're all invited to my welcome-back party for Joe. And, given his impeccable taste for the finer things, the party will be lunch today at one of Joe's and my favorite restaurants, namely Sancho's Taco Shop. I've arranged for a buffet of Sancho's gourmet specialties. It's scheduled for one-thirty 'til three this afternoon. That'll ensure that the restaurant will be virtually empty by the time we get there. And the hour and a half will allow you guys to come and go in shifts so Jasper Creek doesn't become one big crime scene while all of JC's finest are stuffing their faces at the same time."

Everyone expressed their appreciation for the lunch invitation. All but two department members, even the chief, made it to Sancho's and enjoyed the food and camaraderie.

Back home that evening, Joe and Ginny began their "get reacquainted" program. "Wow, Ginny. Looks like you've settled in well here. Any second thoughts about having sold your condo?"

"What condo?" asked Ginny as she smiled.

A nice dinner cooked by Ginny, some more discussions while cuddled together on the living room couch, a night together in bed and their getting-reacquainted program was well along by breakfast the next morning.

Chapter 50

With the chief's approval, Joe and Ginny took the next day off, primarily to give Joe time to settle back in and do whatever personal errands he had to catch up on.

"OK, Joe. This is our three-day weekend. Let's not blow it. Let's organize how we want to spend our time."

"Good idea. I suggest we make three lists: work related, personal stuff to get done and personal enjoyment stuff."

"Works for me. But when the lists are finished, I bet we'll need more than just this weekend."

"Probably right, but we gotta start someplace."

"Let's start with the work stuff. I want to hear every detail of your time on the task force. I know the headlines, but now I want the nitty-gritty details."

"Fair enough. And I'll add the same topic for all that you and Denny did while I was away. Plus, a briefing on your current cases, which I assume I'll be jumping into starting Monday morning. But, first, I want to thank you for that welcome lunch at Sancho's. I was really surprised and touched by it."

"You're very welcome. I'm looking forward to us being partners again. I mean, Denny was great, but he isn't you."

"And we have to add a discussion, or maybe several discussions, on that 'thing.' Not sure if it belongs here or under personal things."

"You mean the —"

"Yes, exactly. Your feeling that I'm always, I don't know what, overpowering you, I guess, when we work cases. And also in deciding personal stuff. I was shocked when you first mentioned it. We couldn't really discuss this or do much about it, other than my not offering suggestions about your cases while I was away. But now that I'm back, we need to really discuss this in detail."

"I'm glad you feel that way. Let's list this under 'personal' even though it covers both work and personal stuff."

"OK. Also under personal, we need to list house hunting and planning our wedding. If that's still what you want, of course."

"Joe! How can you even ask that? Of course, it's still what I want. If anything, your being away made me realize all the more how much I love you. I really missed you."

"Glad to hear that. That overpowering thing has me a bit spooked."

"Joe, how could you have doubted it for a second?"

"I don't know. I guess, being a cop for so long, my mind automatically focuses on the worst possible outcomes."

"Yeah, well, that doesn't apply to stuff dealing with you and me. Got that?"

"Yes ma'am, I got it and will try to control my brain accordingly."

"Good. What else?"

"I need to tell you all about my feelings about my undercover assignment. Being a rat vs. catching dirty cops. This whole thing is still bugging me."

"Definitely goes on the list. For whatever's bugging you, just think of me as your personal exterminator."

"OK, Miss Terminix. Thanks. By the way, my items for our personal enjoyment list are simple and few in number: walk, nap, cuddle and sex. And not necessarily in that order."

"Works for me. Don't think I can improve on that."

As they both expected, this list of things was not fully accomplished in one day, not even one weekend. Several tasks were completed, while others took days and, in a few cases, weeks to work through. Completed were Joe's detailed descriptions of his task force work and Ginny's descriptions of her and Denny's work, as well as their current open cases.

Some of the personal items on their list were not discussed in detail, but they did agree on the next steps and target dates for each item. They agreed they had to talk through their marriage and house-hunting plans and schedules sooner rather than later. They did manage to successfully complete all the personal enjoyment items that day — taking a walk in a nearby park, followed by cuddling, sex and a nap.

Unfortunately, they spent only a limited amount of time talking about Ginny's feelings of becoming subordinated or suppressed by Joe, when working on a case and even regarding trivial things like what to do for dinner. Joe understood what Ginny said, but couldn't imagine why she had those feelings. They both agreed that this was a very important subject. Not knowing whether Ginny's perceptions were real or imagined, they agreed they needed to find ways to change Joe's actions as well as Ginny's feelings.

The other important topic that was briefly discussed but

put aside for a later date was Joe's task force experiences, his thoughts and resultant actions. Joe briefly described how, in some ways, he preferred the drug task force work over his normal detective work. "As a detective, unless we're trying to find a serial murderer or bomber, we pretty much identify, capture and then prove the guilt of the perp after the fact. Much of the drug work felt more rewarding: Capturing drugs and dealers was preventing future crimes and deaths, not just catching the bad guy after the crime was committed."

"Joe, do you think you want to switch to drug enforcement work going forward?"

"Damned if I know. But probably not. I like the preventing aspect of it, but I can see getting burned out pretty quickly. As soon as you get one of the bad guys off the street, he's immediately replaced by another bum. It's like there's a cast of thousands just waiting for their turn. You can correct a situation with a specific bad dude, but the next equally bad dude jumps right in. This can get old and frustrating pretty quickly. And that's not all."

"Oh?"

"Yeah, there's one more thing. You know how I struggled with being a rat, spying on my fellow officers, in order to put dirty cops away. Well, I'm still struggling with this choice. But it's worse than that."

"Oh, how?"

"Ginny, I was very close to doing something I've never done before. Something I swore to myself that I'd never do and something that I hated whenever I knew another cop had done it."

"Yikes. What did you almost do that was so terrible? It doesn't sound like you, Joe."

"We should wait until we have more time to discuss this. It can wait, even though it has me really upset and confused. But, just to keep you from going crazy wondering, I was close to planting false evidence to be totally sure that agents I one-hundred percent knew were dirty would be convicted."

"Wow."

"My feelings exactly, Ginny. Even though I didn't do it, it still shakes me up to realize how seriously I considered doing it. Anyhow, let's talk more about this when we have more time."

And with that, Joe and Ginny's three-day weekend came to an end. Dinner at a local pizzeria, two TV shows and then off to bed. But they both knew they had a lot left to talk about and deal with in the days and weeks ahead.

Chapter 51

Although they continued their discussions during the week, it wasn't until the next weekend that Joe and Ginny were able to continue their talks in depth. They started right after breakfast on Saturday. They wanted to be sure that they allocated enough time to fully talk through the important topics they hadn't got through yet.

"OK, Ginny, let's start with the topic I so elegantly labeled 'the thing' the other day."

"Agreed. Want me to explain my feelings first?"

"No need. I'm pretty sure I understand what your feelings are. We need to focus on why you feel that way, and what we should do about it."

"OK. I never felt this way, or, if I did, I didn't even realize I did. It started while you were on the task force. The couple of times where I described how Denny and I were totally stuck, you said something or asked the right question that helped get us unstuck."

"And that's bad?"

"No. In fact, it was good. You helped us to start making progress again, and that was good."

"So?"

"After the fact, I realized how he and I couldn't make any progress without your guidance. Even when you couldn't help us come up with some next steps, I felt better about myself just knowing that even you didn't have the answer."

"Ginny, that's not —"

"Well, right or wrong, it was how I felt. Then my brain went hyperactive. Pretty soon, I realized this same relationship was true when you and I worked together. And I realized it even applied to our personal lives — what to have for dinner, which restaurant to go to, and so on."

"Ginny, like I've said, I think you're exaggerating. But what I think in this case doesn't matter. It's what you think about it that counts."

"Joe, I —"

"Hold on. Please. I wasn't finished. Ginny, since you first told me this, I feel like I'm walking on eggshells whenever we're together. And even when we spoke on the phone. I'm so focused on not saying the wrong thing, I think I miss half of our conversations."

"Joe, I'm sorry."

"Ginny, you shouldn't apologize. You didn't do anything wrong. Like it or not, your brain thinks what it wants to think."

"So, what do we do about it, Joe?"

"Damned if I know. I'm hoping that time, now that I'm back, will gradually get us back to where we were. Especially if I watch what I say."

"Joe, you shouldn't have to live that way."

"It's a small price to pay if it works. But there is the chance that it doesn't get better. Ginny, I love you more than I can describe and I couldn't wait for the task force assignment to end so I could get back here full-time with you. Hell, the initially estimated, OK guesstimated, eight months turned into a damn full year plus. But, despite my dying to be back here, I think we need to hold off on the house and marriage stuff until we see how this turns out."

"My God! Joe, are you saying you don't want us to live together, much less get married?"

"No, I'm just saying we should hold off until this 'thing' gets resolved. In fact, if we knew at the time, it might have been better to have held off on you selling your condo."

"Joe? Do you want me to move out?"

"No! Definitely not. It's just that we'd have more options open to us if you still had the condo. As a minimum, you used to like spending an occasional night there just to take a short break from us being constantly together. I'm sorry I kept pushing you to sell it sooner rather than later."

"Joe, selling it was a decision that we both made. Together."

After holding back her tears with all her strength, Ginny lost it. But only briefly. She choked off her crying, wiped her eyes and blew her nose.

"Sorry about that. Don't know what got into me."

"No need to apologize. You're upset. I get that. Especially given my clumsy explanation."

"Thanks, Joe. I don't feel very well right now. OK if I go take a nap?"

"Sure. Go ahead. Just please don't misread what I've been saying. Go take your nap, and we'll continue later."

Ginny was surprised when Joe woke her at noon.

"OK, sleepy head, time to get up."

"Jeez, I had no idea I'd sleep the morning away. I woke several times, but each time I fell back within a couple of minutes."

"Good. Time for lunch. I opened a can of tomato soup, to be followed by tuna and tomatoes. With a beer or two, of course."

"Thanks, Joe."

Ginny felt a bit better than she had before her nap, but she was still petrified that her life was about to fall apart.

"Joe, I'm sorry I ever mentioned this to you."

"Ginny, don't go there. I'm glad you did. You had to. Not talking about it would be almost like lying to me. In fact, it would be a lie. Of omission. We need to tell each other everything. That's the only way we even have a chance of fixing it."

"You're right. So, after lunch, let's dive into your task force issues."

"Will do."

Forty minutes later, they were sitting on the living room couch, each with a just-opened cold bottle of beer in their hands.

"Joe, I fully get what you said about the task force work preventing crimes and deaths, compared to us usually working on crimes after they happen."

"Exactly. And with the softer and softer prosecutors and judges, even many of the perps we capture and help convict are back out on the street almost by the time we've walked from the courthouse back to our desks. And then we wonder why we sometimes get frustrated."

"Not sure I'm ready for a career change, but you describe my feelings perfectly. Now let's talk about those evidence-planting temptations."

"Yeah. There my thinking's a bit mixed up. Hell, it's more like scrambled eggs than a bit mixed up. I've never planted evidence, and I got real pissed whenever I found out or suspected that another cop did. Even when I worked in Chicago, where it was SOP for many cops and sergeants."

"So what was different this time?"

"Not sure. I think it was that I view dirty law enforcement folks as worse than most any type of criminal. They're the worst of the worst. And I wanted to be sure that the bad ones were convicted. Not have a good chance of being convicted, but being positive the evidence wouldn't let them off the hook. And when I worried we didn't have solid enough evidence, I thought about — and actually planned how — I could fake it."

"Are you sorry that you did?"

"That's just it. I don't know. I think so. I know it's wrong and something I always hated others doing, but, at the same time, it felt good to think that I could make sure the bad agents would be convicted."

"Joe, I can understand your feeling that way, but you should feel good that your true nature won out and you didn't act on your thoughts."

"That's for sure. But I'm still shook with how tempted I was. And how close I came."

"Joe, I think that's just human nature. No different than a married man looking at a pretty woman walking by and fantasizing spending the night with her. As long as the fantasizing doesn't happen too frequently and, of course, doesn't lead to them actually spending the night together, it's no harm-no foul in my view."

"I know. You're right. Just wanted to share this 'cause we're partners in everything, and I still feel bad about my fake-evidence fantasy."

"Glad to hear that, Joe. That just shows once again what a great person you are."

"Thanks. OK, I say that's it for now. Let's just give all this some time. No major decisions, just let time do its thing for now."

"OK. You got a deal there partner," said Ginny as she stuck her right hand out. "It's scary, but it's the right thing to do."

Joe shook Ginny's hand. The handshake gradually evolved into a strong hug and a deep, long kiss.

Born in Brooklyn, NY, Stuart has lived in 7 states and 4 European countries. He and his wife now live in the foothills of the Blue Ridge Mountains. Stuart earned an engineering degree from Swarthmore College and an MBA from Harvard University. His career has included work for large multinational firms, small startups and management consulting firms. Stuart and his wife are instrument-rated private pilots and Stuart is a volunteer firefighter & EMT and a Red Cross Disaster Responder.

See what Stuart Safft is up to at his blog: https://stuartsafft.wordpress.com.

Other Books from Stuart Safft

Where's Ellen?
A Joe McFarland / Ginny Harris Mystery

Body in the Warehouse
A Joe McFarland / Ginny Harris Mystery

Killed at Home
A Joe McFarland / Ginny Harris Mystery

Cold Cargo
A Joe McFarland / Ginny Harris Mystery